Dear
Entrepreneur

Letters from those that have made it and are making it happen

By Danny Bailey & Andrew Blackman

A Brightword book
www.brightwordpublishing.com

HARRIMAN HOUSE LTD
3A Penns Road
Petersfield
Hampshire
GU32 2EW
GREAT BRITAIN

Tel: +44 (0)1730 233870
Fax: +44 (0)1730 233880
Email: enquiries@harriman-house.com
Website: www.harriman-house.com
First published in Great Britain in 2013.
Copyright © Harriman House Ltd

The rights of Danny Bailey and Andrew Blackman to be identified as Authors has been
asserted in accordance with the Copyright, Design and Patents Act 1988.

ISBN: 978-1-908003-54-6

British Library Cataloguing in Publication Data
A CIP catalogue record for this book can be obtained from the British Library.

Book printed and bound in the UK by Lightning Source

Set in ACaslon Regular and HVD Bodedo Medium

Contents

About Danny and Andrew

Danny Bailey is a highly motivated 9-5 guy that loves thinking up new ideas and fiddling around with the backend of websites. He came up with the idea of *Dear Entrepreneur* by putting together his knowledge of publishing and business. He is a keen middle distance runner and general fitness fanatic.

Andrew Blackman is a final year university student studying Finance and Business. Having made his mind up at an early age that working in an office from 9-5 was not for him, he has actively pursued alternative avenues. His aim is to start his own company once he graduates. He is a very keen sailor and football spectator.

You can follow Danny and Andrew on Twitter **@DearTrep** and read more at **www.dearentrepreneur.co.uk**.

Introduction

Hi, my name is Danny **and my name is Andrew.**

We are the same as you.

I have never started a business but have always had the ambition to. I have always done the 'normal' thing of working 9-5 and moaning about not having enough money. I never had the motivation to get off my arse and change things – until now.

I decided to ask people that have started businesses how I should go about starting up and also to ask for any advice they could give me. After receiving an amazing response, and having worked in publishing for most of my working life, I decided to publish their advice in a book for the world to see.

I don't mind working 9-5, I actually quite like it, but my issue is the future and how I can make extra money to enjoy my personal life; I suppose it's about working to live rather than living to work. **I am the youngest of three. I am a final year university student studying Finance and Business with the ambition never to start the 9-5 slog. Ever since I can remember I have wanted to be my own boss. I have never envisaged myself working the normal 9-5; I just don't think it is for me. I'm not the kind of person who ponders over things for a long time. I usually go on gut instinct and give 100% commitment, or I just don't bother.**

Business in general is a topic I enjoy and I guess that is why I have continued to study it. I was under the impression you needed a degree to get somewhere in life, however the more I have thought about it the more I start to question it. What is worth more, a degree or four years experience on my CV? I am not really sure anymore.

The thought of working for somebody else doesn't motivate me or get me excited. Who would be reaping the rewards for all my hard work and effort? It wouldn't be me. I need more to motivate me than a fixed monthly pay slip. I love the idea of creating and nurturing an idea into something I am proud of. I relish the thought of having the flexibility to work when I want to and having the responsibility to make the decisions.

I haven't really done that much with my life so far. I'm a 21-year-old who hasn't particularly stepped off the increasingly routine educational path. For my placement year I worked in London – which was pretty cool and an extremely useful experience – but the four-hour a day commute was torture and did almost kill me. Sitting on a train for almost 20 hours a week gave me a lot of thinking time:

Do I really want to be stuck in an office every day for the rest of my life from 9am to 5pm?

The answer was a categorical NO. In all honesty I can't really get my head around the thought of giving up 40+ years of my life to be part of a corporate machine, being a numbered part in a well-oiled engine. I guess this might be where I differ. But then perhaps not, as YOU have chosen to pick up this book…

I am quite different to Andrew. He wants to be the next Alan Sugar or Peter Jones (nothing wrong with that!), but I have quite different ambitions. To me, achievements are completing the Marathon des Sables, the Three Peaks Challenge, an Iron Man or cycling from Land's End to John o'Groats. What I aim for is to be able to achieve these things – and believe it or not they cost money (why would someone pay to do these things?!) I know it sounds crazy but I love the feeling I get when completing these types of challenges. My entrepreneurial side funds the things I enjoy doing. It's not about making a billion pounds or having offices in every major city in the world, it's about having the financial freedom to live the life I want.

What I am trying to say is that while it is great to aim high, also aim for what you want and with the right attitude you will achieve it, against all odds. Read inspiring books, listen to motivational speeches, anything that will change your attitude and get you motivated to achieve what you want. You will never be happy until you know what you want out of life. Remember, we aren't here for a long time; we're here for a GOOD TIME!

This is the start of what we hope to be both your journey and ours. Remember, it is never too late or too early, lessons will be learnt and adventures will be had. We hope that this manages to help you on your way. Enjoy.

Foreword

Dear Entrepreneur,

IT WOULD HAVE BEEN USEFUL having a book like this when I was starting my first business!

Congratulations to Danny and Andrew for encouraging so many successful entrepreneurs to pass on their secrets of success – that's an entrepreneurial endeavour in its own right!

Stories from entrepreneurs such as Kate Castle of BoginaBog (the lady I refer to as the most glamorous girl in toilets!), Richard Reed of Innocent and Mark Rock of Audioboo serve to inspire and inform. They are brought together in an easy to read style and I defy anyone not to pick up a tip or two from these pages.

Some common themes emerge from the entrepreneurs with the key message being: do what you love, surround yourself with good people, take care of customers, and excel at marketing. The profiled entrepreneurs show how it's done and talk about the feelings they experienced along the way.

With its keepsake stories and words of advice, this is a welcome addition to the reading list for any start-up or growing business.

Emma Jones

Founder of Enterprise Nation (**www.enterprisenation.com**) and co-founder of StartUp Britain (**www.startupbritain.org**)

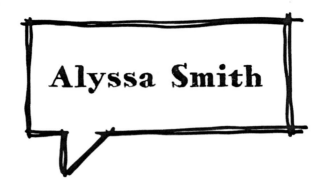

Alyssa Smith

Dear Entrepreneur,

IT IS SO IMPORTANT FOR BUSINESSES TO GET NOTICED and stand out from the crowd in any positive way they can. It's such a crowded market out there, and my advice to anyone wanting to start up a business who perhaps does not have funding, investment or much in the way of start up funds would be to make yourself different and make your business stand out. Social media as a powerful and free marketing tool is very important, as it can help you reach a worldwide audience and tell people about your business who may not otherwise find you.

I also have lots of celebrities who endorse my products, which is again free publicity, and a very effective way of marketing. If you are looking to have endorsements from celebrities, my advice would be to choose carefully, and use someone who will reflect your company or brand in a positive way.

When I started my business, I made the most of any free PR available to me, frequently offering to write for magazines and newspapers, which is a great way of getting your name out there, and for free. Magazines are usually interested in your story as long as the angle and content is interesting and relevant to their readers, so this is something to bear in mind.

Anyone who thinks that starting a business is easy is completely wrong. Before you start your business, make sure that you are ready for some serious hurdles and are very thick skinned. It's hard, but if you have fire in your belly and the passion and determination to succeed, you can!

Alyssa Smith

Founder and director, Alyssa Smith   *Alyssa Smith*
www.alyssasmith.co.uk

Audioboo

Dear Entrepreneur,

Both you and I aren't very special or iconic manifestations of the beauty of the free market. We are often misfits, beneficiaries of inherited wealth or education or just plain lucky. My last business – which sold for $60m after four years – happened because my builder talked to the builder of my future partner. Never underestimate the role of serendipity in success, despite everything else that may be stacked against you.

There is maybe a right way to do this start-up thing and a number of wrongs ways. Most of which I have probably tried. I am imbued with a sense of optimism over the most ridiculous ideas. Remind me to tell you one day about the themed pizza delivery business (Margherita's delivered by a girl called Margherita, American Hot delivered by... well you get the picture!). It never got off the ground. Nor the Love Egg you could use to relay your email. And. And. And.

So read on with that in mind and take what you need and leave the rest behind.

❝ Never underestimate the role of serendipity in success. ❞

1. **Embrace failure** since it shows you what you should be doing right. There is nothing wrong with making bad decisions if the only other option is not to make a decision at all. Creating new stuff is very Darwinion and natural selection will easily cull the ideas that can't or won't work.

2. **Hire people that are better than you.** A very simple rule that builds great teams. And great teams build great businesses.

3. **If you don't ask, you don't get.** Suggest opportunities to people you want to work with. Then suggest again. And again. It may piss them off but it hasn't cost you anything but your pride. And sometimes, just sometimes, they may finally say yes.

4. **Be nice.** You don't have to be a wanker or a bully to succeed. It may help in the short term but it doesn't make anyone's life any easier or richer. Including your own.

5. **Be good.** Always think what you can do to help others if your idea works. It's great to be successful and hopefully be rich. It's also better to know that you have the power to affect a change – in one person's life or in a nations' – that someone working for a company can never do.

6. **Don't fret about valuation when raising money.** If investors are going to shaft you then they will find an opportunity regardless of how much you stand up to them. That's called having the wrong investors. Just focus on the opportunity you may miss if you obsess with a perceived value.

7. **Change the plan when you have to.** The first soldiers on Utah Beach on D-Day in 1944 were blown off course and considerably south of their landing point. They could have manoeuvred slowly back to where the plan stated. Instead they landed where they were and famously stated, "We'll start the war from here!" Do the same.

8. **Have fun.** Or try your best to have fun. Or, at the very least, wake up in the morning hoping you're going to have at least a slight bit of fun. Despite the pressure and pain of starting something new, when you don't enjoy it anymore it's a sign it's time to sell out or move on.

9. **Stay close to your family and friends.** Being an entrepreneur is the loneliest job in the world. You need the people that love you despite yourself to stay dear to you.

10. And finally, **believe in yourself.** Because a lot of the time no one else will until a certain moment in time is reached. It was William Gibson who said, "The future has already arrived — it's just not evenly distributed yet." You may just have to wait a bit longer than you thought for your success and vision to shine through.

Regards, and watching out for your future success that ignores each point here.

Mark Rock
Founder & CEO, Audioboo Ltd
www.audioboo.fm

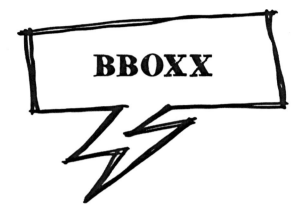

Dear Entrepreneur,

ASSUMING YOU HAVE A GOOD IDEA:

- Get a great contact network – reality check: whatever you plan to achieve probably can't be done on your own. Get to know people in your proposed industry or even supporting industries that you could call on at a later date. Go to those cheesy networking events where even though it feels like everybody is interested in self-promotion, you may just find that interested party that will serve you well in the future.

- Get a buzz going about your product/service – enter competitions, speak to the media at every opportunity, get a great website and social media presence – all will help raise your profile without costing a ridiculous amount.

- Work frigging hard – some of our team worked two jobs to get the business off the ground; most people in these pages probably did the same. Expect to work 80+ hours a week if you want to make a new venture a sustainable success. If your idea is good enough then long hours will probably mean success.

- Know your customers – and this applies not just to the people you are selling to but also the potential people who may be investing in you. Go and meet them on a regular basis rather then send them countless emails they will read and forget.

- Develop a balanced team with different skills – initially you will do everything and anything for your business, probably because there is not many of you. However, there comes a point where you need to focus on certain tasks that generate the most revenue – employing people with the key skills your business needs, be it in marketing, engineering or logistics etc is crucial and allows you to concentrate on making the only thing that matters at the end of the day: sales.

- Make use of mobile tech and flexible working – if your business allows it, you don't need an expensive office. If you can do everything on a phone/tablet, sat in a coffee shop abusing the free wi-fi, then you can slash your monthly costs and spend money where it really matters.

- Finally, don't be afraid to modify your plans if it doesn't work out – if you can recognise when something is not going to be the success you thought it was (we had plenty of those!), don't be scared to change tack and try again in another direction.

Christopher Baker-Brian

Co-Founder, BBOXX Ltd
www.bboxx.co.uk

the right energy.

Bigger Feet

Dear Entrepreneur,

What would you advise yourself if you could go back to the day you started your business?

Be much smarter with the marketing! I should have made sure I kept a record of all the customers so I could have done a much more effective job of marketing to them and tracking customer behaviour – I definitely think using that sort of data for insight is invaluable for customer-facing businesses. I would have also been much smarter in terms of pricing and branding – I should have positioned the site as much more premium and charged more!

What inspired you to start a business?

I couldn't find shoes for my size 13 feet and thought that there must be a better way to do this! My mum and a family friend helped me with the legal stuff, and then I was off! In fairness, I had experience running a mobile disco and so was comfortable with the idea of starting something new, so it was just a case of spotting a new niche really.

Why start a business and not work for someone else?

I think for me, there were a number of reasons. I wanted some pocket money and I thought this would be more fun than waiting tables or mowing lawns! Then there was a real desire to get some proper business experience, which I had always wanted. I think starting your own business is also a lot of fun and you do get a sense of adventure which I don't think is possible when working for someone else, because you are 100% accountable for everything that goes wrong!

Is it possible to start from scratch?

Yes. Bootstrapping is a well-known practice, and frankly if you're getting into a business which requires huge upfront investment then you should probably look at doing things another way or looking at another opportunity – startups have such a high failure rate that you can't afford to commit too much financially at the beginning if you don't have to!

Do you have any daily routines that make things run smoother?

I make a to-do list, and – crucially – order that to-do list as the time between tasks can be a huge time consumer! Apart from that, I'm focussed and don't procrastinate – if you work solidly and with focus you can get lots done and still have a life!

Oliver Bridge

Founder, Bigger Feet Ltd
www.biggerfeet.com

Blackberry Cottage Fayre

Dear Entrepreneur,

THE DEFINITION OF AN ENTREPRENEUR is "an enterprising individual who builds capital through risk and/or initiative".

I would have never classified myself as either enterprising or a risk taker.

If someone asked me to define myself I would have probably said a quiet person, who maybe lacked confidence that had an idea, and decided one day that it should be acted upon to see where it went. Maybe I am also a little quirky, or should that just be a unique individual.

However, when I talk about my business, I am a different person, I am that enterprising individual, I have that initiative, and I AM THAT RISK TAKER!!!!! Ok, I probably wouldn't go that far.

I set up Blackberry Cottage Fayre, Cakes with Secret Ingredients (Vegetables), in September 2011. So what can I tell you my reader?

- Believe in your business. I am told I am infectious, obviously not in a diseased way but because of my enthusiasm. I tell everyone I meet about my business as you never know who you might tell that has a connection somewhere. For instance, I was telling my hairdresser about an award that I was through to the final for – a Best Product Award – and little did I know that one of his clients was setting up a coffee shop and was looking for "different" cakes. He spoke to her about me and a couple of days later I was having meetings. The same hairdresser told another client who ran a village community shop, which also lead to another outlet.

- One of the hardest lessons I have learnt is the ability to say no! Never be afraid to say no, sometimes it is the right thing to say.

- Have a book beside the bed. Lots of my ideas or thoughts happen at strange times, and you can never remember them in the morning, or if you do then you haven't had a decent night's sleep.

- Gut instinct is a funny one, but if something doesn't feel right then it probably won't be right so consider it carefully. Too many times I have acted against my gut instinct and have ended up in the mire wishing I had listened to it in the first place.

- Never jump into something, instead sit back for a little bit, maybe an hour or two or even a day or two. It may be an email you need to send, a quote (leave plenty of time to fill them in and keep re-reading) or a reply to a letter, but you will often go back to it and see mistakes, or think 'should I really say that?'.

- On saying that I am not a risk taker, sometimes you need to take a risk or two, but just keep it realistic; you are already a risk taker for setting your business up.

- I was given a good bit of advice when I was setting up initially: go for awards, it will give you great publicity (and it does).

- Use your support network. You will need them, even if it is a friend who has offered a hand leafleting, manning a stall, or in my case babysitting whilst I had an important meeting. Your network will love to be asked if they have offered to help.

- In your support network try and have people that are also setting up businesses. It is a great journey to have together, and when you are feeling rubbish and things are not going right they will be there for you as you will for them in the same situation.

- Keep your plan to hand so you keep yourself focused, as it is all too easy to get side tracked. Do listen to your clients/customers – you need them!

- If an area of the business is becoming hard to achieve then it may be that you do not have the necessary skills to achieve it. This doesn't mean that you have been defeated, just know your limitations. It may that be you need a specialist in that area, leaving you to concentrate on what you are good at: your business.

So with all that in mind, if you are reading this then you are probably one step nearer to starting up your new business. Good luck and go for it. Remember all you need is PHD: Passion, Hard work and Determination.

Good luck,

Kate Saunders

Founder, of Blackberry Cottage Fayre
www.blackberrycottagefayre.co.uk

Dear Entrepreneur,

You need to want it more

Starting your own company is one of the hardest, but most rewarding challenges you will take on. To succeed where other people have stumbled, you need to want it more than the next guy. This can prove to be the difference between succeeding and failing.

I truly believe that Blackcircles.com grew to what it is today largely due to the fact that I just wanted it more than some of my competitors.

Be prepared to take risks

Risk taking is perhaps the most dangerous part of owning a company, but it is also the most exciting. If your business is to grow and thrive, you will have to perform some calculated risks.

People are often afraid to take a risk as they don't think that it will pay off. Even if this is the case, by experiencing small failures we learn to get back on our feet and come back with more determination and a better idea of how you will succeed next time. Taking risks is a vital part of owning a business.

Make use of all available resources

If there is something that can help you, take advantage of it – from an expert in their field giving you some advice, to applying for a business grant. Whatever is offered to you, make sure to grab it with both hands.

Any help that you can gain along the way will seem like a godsend when you first start. These opportunities can be rare and they won't come to you, you've got to get out there and find them.

Network, network and network again

Thriving business owners are generally also fantastic networkers. Navigating through the minefield of owning a company without friends is not impossible, but it can be a lot harder.

By meeting other entrepreneurs, you can share your experiences, achievements and obstacles. Through networking, you have the opportunity to tap into a vast collection of knowledge, as well as the chance to gain deals in sectors you may have not even considered before.

Be prepared to adapt

Adapting to circumstances can be uncomfortable for some people. There are times when it does not matter how much you have researched a topic, how encompassing your strategy is, or how much you believe in your plan – you will have to change something to deal with external factors you had not factored in.

If you can learn to adapt and roll with the punches, you will be able to weather any potential storms.

Michael Welch

Founder, Blackcircles.com
www.blackcircles.com

blackcircles.com
the new way to new tyres

Blessing M

Dear Entrepreneur,

ENTREPRENEURSHIP IS A REALLY IMPORTANT ISSUE, and something that is becoming increasingly noticed due to the recession and young people struggling with employment. Being an entrepreneur is about more than just starting a business or two, it is about having attitude and the drive to succeed in business.

All successful entrepreneurs have a similar way of thinking and possess several key personal qualities that make them so successful in business. Successful entrepreneurs like the ambitious Richard Branson have an inner drive to succeed and grow their business.

My name is Blessing Maregere; I am a 19-year-old multi-award winning young entrepreneur. I started my first business at the age of 16, which was a contract cleaning company called Essential Cleaning Company. This was back in 2009 when I had finished my GCSE exams and couldn't find a job, so I decided to create my own.

I had six staff working for me and a number of cleaning contracts and my early success motivated me to set up another business called Bright Futures Enterprise, a social enterprise with a mission to inspire, educate and motivate young people to become successful entrepreneurs.

I sold my cleaning company after a year as I wanted to do more challenging things and I launched Not Just a Youth Enterprise in 2011 with my business partners. Not Just a Youth Enterprise is a youth-led social enterprise and we have developed our own brand of Fairtrade products ranging from rice and chocolate to coffee, tea and hot chocolate.

How to get started when you don't know where to begin and 3 steps to success

A lot of young people want to become their own boss but don't know where to begin. But I believe it's possible for any young person to follow their dreams and do what they love.

Before starting my first business I was volunteering at community youth groups with a helping hand from organisations like vInspired. Volunteering provided me with a whole new network of people and organisations who believe in young people's potential.

Through a combination of experience and networking, I developed the confidence and belief to get out there and give things a go. I believe anyone can become an entrepreneur if they put their mind to it. For any young people out there who want to set up their own business or start a youth project, here are my 3 top tips to get your ideas off the ground:

1. Network

Networking is the key to success – it's not about what you know, it's who you know. So get out there and network with likeminded people; you never know which invaluable contact or person you might meet.

2. Seek a business mentor

Going solo can be lonely, so having a mentor is key to help guide your business to success. It could be a business contact, or even a friend or family member to bounce your ideas off – having someone to provide

you with moral support, guidance and encouragement can make a world
of difference.

3. Passion

Do what you love and love what you do! You need passion to make your
dreams a success – without passion it will never work. Choose to work
on the things that are really important to you – if you care about them
enough, you'll stick with them.

Blessing Maregere

Founder & Chair,
Not Just A Youth Enterprise
www.notjustawebsite.org.uk

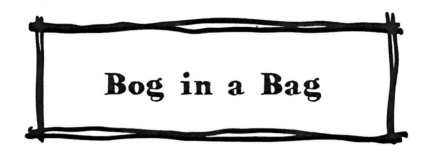

Bog in a Bag

Dear Entrepreneur,

CONTAINED WITHIN THIS LETTER are the key learnings that have lead me to be where I am today. Some I have been lucky enough to stumble across but most I know simply because I got it wrong the first time! So let's start with that…

1. Be prepared to make mistakes – I have lost money and sleep over taking the wrong path. This is inevitable there is no ten-stage plan to launching a great business. It is simply how we deal with these mistakes that determines whether you are an entrepreneur.

2. Love what you do – Even if, like BoginaBag, it may not appear glamorous you have to believe 100% that you have what the market needs. Throughout your journey you will meet people who doubt your product or service.

3. Understand your numbers – Your idea might be great but if you don't understand your cash flow, profit and gross/net margins you will not have a business.

4. Listen to others – Meet, connect and blog with as many people in business as you can. This will not only give you a network of valuable

connections but will also keep you sane. Being an entrepreneur can be lonely, especially in the early days.

5. Limit costs – At the start keep your day job, work from home and outsource everything. Costs can escalate easily and any profit will be hard to earn.

6. Take risks ("who dares wins") – No entrepreneur ever got to be successful by taking the easy path. Put yourself on the line and if you aren't willing to do that then you haven't got #2 sorted. *Dragons' Den* was terrifying but it took my business to the next level.

7. Never be complacent – Understand your customer, exceed their expectations and listen when they say you have got something wrong.

8. Know your limitations – Try everything from managing accounts to pulling in sales, but be realistic. If it isn't working then bring in others that can make it happen.

9. Have fun – Finally, remember why you started and focus on where you want to be.

Good luck,

Kate Castle

Inventor and Director, BoginaBag
www.boginabag.com

Booking Bug

Dear Entrepreneur,

I'VE ALWAYS BELIEVED THAT YOU SHOULD ENJOY WORK. In an average job you spend half your waking day at it, for the largest portion of your life. Now I'm aware that being able to enjoy your job is a privilege, and certainly not one many people get, but if you can, if it's possible, you should always try and do a job you enjoy.

As an entrepreneur, however, this becomes not just a nice-to-have, but absolutely vital. Completely critical to your success is the fact that you need to enjoy your normal day-to-day work. To build your business and to inspire others, if you can't be upbeat and genuinely excited about what you do, then no-one else will be either.

When your idea is new, like a new love, everything is exciting. But once that first excitement has faded, what are you left with? I've known entrepreneurs who are always seeking the excitement of a new idea and a new project, but lose interest once they hit the daily grind of actually building a business. They may be lucky one day and hit upon something that makes it big quick enough before they lose interest, but the truth is that most businesses are built with hard work, sweat and tears over a longer period of time; years, not months.

The question is never "are you excited and enthusiastic about your business?" on day one, or day ten – that's easy – but what about by day 100, or day 1,000? Three years into building your business will you still have the same puppy dog enthusiasm? Maybe, or maybe not, but that's not important. What is important, what you absolutely must do, without question is really, really enjoy it.

I'm not talking about the occasional highs or lows, but the day-to-day activities, whatever it is that actually fills your waking hours with the building of the vision you're creating, and the role you fulfil in shaping it. That could be anything from writing code to waiting tables, managing staff, or just having meetings and writing emails; whatever day-to-day role you take in your business. You have to love it, and not just when it's new, but when you're years in. If it's a burden, if it's a hassle, if you'd rather stay in bed, then this will show. Your staff will see it, your clients, your investors; it will be written plain across your face if you are not actually enjoying what you do. You can't fake it, it's not about having a smile on the outside while you're crying on the inside; it needs to be genuine. Enjoy what you do and it will show to everyone around you.

After a bad day, when you got turned down for investment, some new competitor launched, or any one of myriad of setbacks that befall any business, you're going to be depressed. The level of stress that building a business creates is huge, and not for the faint of heart. However, the enthusiasm you inject into your colleagues, your team, your friends, your family, is like a bank you can draw down on later. You're going to have bad days, everyone does, that's not a problem and you don't have to hide them. If you have a good team and good colleagues, they will see this, they will recognise this is not the normal you, they will work to help you pick yourself back up, they will reflect back the enthusiasm you normally show on every other day.

❝Completely critical to your success is the fact that you need to enjoy your normal day-to-day work.❞

At various times you're probably going to question yourself, ask yourself what you are doing and why you are doing it. The what, I can't begin to answer, but the why should be easy, and it's not just as simple as to become rich.

It should be because you really love what you do.

Glenn Shoosmith

CEO & co-founder,
Booking Bug Limited
www.bookingbug.com

Nigel Botterill

Dear Entrepreneur,

WHO YOU HANG AROUND WITH MATTERS. A lot. I used to play a lot of golf when I was younger. What I found was that I always played better when I played golfers who were better than me. Similarly, whenever I played with people who weren't as good as me, I never played to my best. It's a bit like that in business.

Local networking events can be incredibly useful. You meet people, forge relationships and help each other to develop and grow. However, there were some that would go to every single networking event who are not, by any definition, successful. They are stuck in their rut and if you spend too much time with them, then you'll become like them.

In short, if you mix with losers, you become a loser.

If you spend time with super successful business owners, then your chances of achieving the same increase dramatically.

It was the late, great Jim Rohn who said that you become a combination of the five people you spend most time with. Make sure that you're spending time with the right people. People that inspire you, that motivate you, that fuel your ambition and drive and who you can learn from. Being around such people can make a heck of a difference to your level of success.

I was at least twelve months too late in realising this and it held me back a lot in those early months. Please don't make the same mistake that I did.

❝If you mix with losers, you become a loser. ❞

Nigel

www.nigelbotterill.com

Nigel Botterill's
Entrepreneur's
CIRCLE

Nigel Botterill is one of Britain's most successful entrepreneurs. In the last eight years he has built, from scratch, eight separate million-pound plus businesses, and his Entrepreneur's Circle guides and mentors teach thousands of UK business owners who aspire to super success. It is the largest membership organisation in the UK dedicated to helping businesses grow.

Braant

BRADLEY MCLOUGHLIN SOLD SANDWICHES at school, buying cheaper lunches to pocket the difference.

After A-levels in Business Studies, IT and Music Technology, Bradley worked for his Granddad, saving up for a one-month travel ticket to visit London. Armed with a suit and leather folder, every day he walked into various companies blagging his way in to see the HR Director, pretending to reception that he had an appointment!

After finding a job as an Accounts Assistant, Bradley worked in London for eight years, finally ending as a Management Accountant for a large corporate.

With the experience of managing businesses from a financial perspective, Bradley started his own, Trading4u. In five years, turnover reached over £1m and Bradley successfully exited the business.

Bradley's current venture is a London bookkeeping and accountancy business named Braant, which provides professional, reputable and reliable accounting services to SMEs.

What makes you an entrepreneur?

- Being relentless in your goals
- Overcoming every challenge, and not to let it stop you
- Being completely driven on success
- Calculating risk
- Not always following traditional/conventional methods

What inspired you to start a business?

Reward – self-satisfaction and financial.

Self-satisfaction comes before financial quite simply because someone starting a business purely to make money will achieve less compared to someone who completely lives and breathes their venture. Those who completely love what they do will often make money as a by-product of their success.

Money doesn't make you happy, it's the people and achievements in life that does. And if you're a true entrepreneur you will use money as a tool to invest in more ventures, ideas and passions that will yield you more knowledge and self-satisfaction.

I was always inspired by people who'd built up their own companies, in what they had achieved by creating great brands and services, and sometimes changing the way we do things for the better! All I read are entrepreneurs' autobiographies.

I understood at a very young age what a margin was, and more importantly, how to make it. To this day it gives me a great buzz when a deal completes successfully. Of course, the bigger the better and you can then invest the profits into larger opportunities.

However, you have to take the rough with the smooth. It's about calculating your financial and commercial risks, weighing up the pros and cons. As long as overall, most of the time your activity delivers positive results then your risk management is in balance.

66 Money doesn't make you happy, it's the people and achievements in life that does. 99

Is it possible to start from scratch and do you have any tips?

Absolutely, and platforms such as Google, social media, directories, email marketing and your own site certainly provide opportunities to start and grow most businesses.

Here are some tips:

- At the beginning DO NOT tie yourself into lengthy contracts

- Everything is negotiable. Negotiate EVERYTHING!

- Start to use Google AdWords. You can even set your own daily budget

- Don't waste money on marketing unless you comprehensively target your potential clients

- Set your marketing spend as a % of gross margin

- Track marketing spend against income to calculate which marketing channels produce an ROI

- Get comprehensive insurance including legal cover – you never know what's around the corner!

- Accept your weaknesses and commission expert suppliers

- Offer an unbelievable discount to your first customers for referring business

Is starting your second business any easier?

You can apply broad experiences to any business, but a bookkeeping and accountancy firm is very different to buying and selling consumer products!

Braant's market share is concentrated in London and all potential clients are businesses as opposed to consumers, so our marketing needs to target them appropriately, via the most efficient channels. Additionally, CPA (Cost Per Acquisition) will be higher as the industry is more expensive to advertise and competition is a factor.

In short, it will be a challenge, but it wouldn't be me unless I was pushing myself!

In its first year, Braant has met its ambitious target and with more aggressive advertising and more services introduced to compliment the core business, Braant is on track to become one of London's best firms.

Bradley Mcloughlin

Founder, Braant and Trading4U
www.braant.co.uk

Dear Entrepreneur,

DESPITE THE RECENT RECESSION OUR COMPANY sales have grown rapidly since our first restaurant opened on Upper Street in August 2007. I wish I could say that we had planned that type of growth and that the road has been easy. Neither is true, but we do believe our success to date has been a by-product of focusing on a few key things.

Define your brand, then seek to continually improve it

The Chilango brand and its future evolution is our most vital asset. We've evolved our brand a few times since inception, and will unleash the next batch of improvements in our new site. When starting out there's a natural temptation to mimic the brand of a bigger player. Resist. You certainly don't have to reinvent every aspect of your business, but if your total proposition isn't unique then your success will be short-lived.

Our guiding light has been the feeling we want to create with every guest that walks through our doors. As we've grown and spoken with guests so has our thinking about what this feeling should be, and ultimately how the brand should reflect and support it.

66 When starting out there's a natural temptation to mimic the brand of a bigger player. Resist. 99

We define our brand across Food, People and Place, and have a set of promises, or benefits, we aim to provide our guests within each area. The sum of these promises create our proposition: We like to think we brighten up people's day.

The best people create the best companies, EVERYTHING else is secondary

People means crew, management, suppliers, creatives, investors...anyone that may have a part in or touch Chilango. Taking the time to find, attract, and reward highly competent, like-minded people means the trust runs high, while the need or want to look over shoulders runs low, and everyone can focus completely on the road ahead.

Our company vision has always been our best currency, whether it's persuading a supplier to work with us sooner rather than later, or getting that highly experienced and talented person to forego the high salary and focus on the equity upside instead.

The best people will always weather the worst storms.

Ignore the naysayers

Quality and value are key words within our brand, and despite the recession we haven't budged on either. Every time we've been able to pocket some additional margin through purchasing scale, we've chosen to share some of the profit back with the customer by upgrading our raw material supply as well. Despite the recessionary marketing tactics of other players, we've generally avoided discounting as we think it will only cheapen the Chilango brand.

Lots of people along the way have strongly advised us against such a strategy. We've certainly looked at ways to save money and cut costs, but cheapening the guest experience is by no means the right way to finance these savings. Ignore anyone who thinks otherwise.

★ ★ ★

Don't get me wrong – the climb to get to where we are today has been a hell of a battle. Most of our new guests have never even had a burrito in their life, or could even accurately describe one. But we've stuck to our guns and can without doubt see the dividends ahead and the light shining at the tunnel's end.

Eric Partaker

Co-Founder and Director, Chilango
www.chilango.co.uk

Chokolit

Dear Entrepreneur,

WHEN I STARTED MY BUSINESS I set myself some principles that I stick to and that help to keep me focused, but despite that, running a business is not straightforward and there are many aspects that you just can't plan. My advice is to be open to changes. Go with the flow as much as you can, but you will come across many obstacles that need a decision that you might not have allowed for in order to move forward. You have to be open to new challenges and opportunities.

Why I started my business

I never felt that I belonged in the educational system and this was a very unhappy time for me. It wasn't until I was 11 years old that finally, after an Educational Psychologist assessment, I was diagnosed with dyslexia, dyspraxia, dyscalculia and short-term memory loss coupled with a high IQ. Although this was a massive relief for me and I did not see it as a disadvantage at all, being taken out of school to be home tutored was a necessity. I was bullied badly and it was a group decision between my family and I.

My love of animals led me to a job at a local falconry centre where I learnt that I had an amazing ability to absorb information, and for the first time was able to read book after book because it was a subject that fascinated me. I also took to speaking publicly with ease and used this new-found skill to talk to the public about the birds at the centre. It was whilst walking through a garden centre at work that I came across a book for sale, *Belgian Chocolates and Cakes*. I bought it and set about absorbing everything I had read. I began to get requests to make chocolate cakes for family and friends and as word spread I seemed to be spending more and more of my time in the kitchen fulfilling orders. As they say, that's when I had the Eureka! moment and decided to turn my passion into a business. The rest is history. To cut a very long story short, I became the youngest supplier to Waitrose at 13, Sainsbury's at 14 and Selfridges at 16.

If you are wondering why my company is called "Chokolit", it came about simply because being dyslexic that is how I spell chocolate. When I needed to come up with a brand name I realised without thinking I already had.

Why to start a business rather than work for someone else

Running your own business is the most rewarding, exciting and exhilarating career you could ever choose but nothing will test your strength, commitment and perseverance more!

I aspire to be a recognised entrepreneur, to grow a global business and to make an impact in my industry and to the lives of young people across the world.

Good luck

Louis Barnett

Founder, Chokolit

www.chokolit.co.uk

CHOCOLATIER

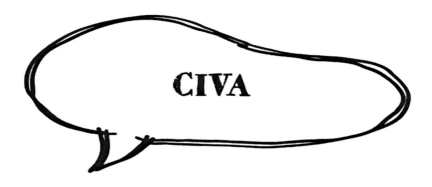

CIVA

Dear Entrepreneur,

HERE ARE SIX BITS OF ADVICE from my experience which I hope you will find useful.

1. **If you have got a good idea for a business, then do something**. A good idea is only a good idea if it leads on to something, and it is up to you to take the first step. The Chinese philosopher Lao Tzu, who was the father of Taoism some 2,500 years ago, said that, "A journey of 1,000 miles begins with a single step". Take that first step, and you're on your way. The next steps will become apparent, and you will learn from experience as you go along. Fail to take that first step, and nothing will happen.

2. **You can learn from failure as much as you can learn from success.** So if things go wrong, sit back and think why. What could you have done differently? How will you turn your failure into success? My favourite quote is from the Irish playwright Samuel Beckett: "No Matter. Try again. Fail again. Fail better."

3. **If you have a problem, think, think, think... and also ask others for their ideas.** Some years back I set up a publishing imprint to produce books for people running charities. I wanted to create something which would generate a lot of income in order to make

the publishing operation sustainable. So I took a hot bath, and started thinking. Could I think of something which people really needed and wanted, which could be sold at a relatively high price, and which would go out of date quite quickly? I thought and thought. And then I had a "Eureka" moment, and like Archimedes I jumped out of the bath with my good idea. It was to publish a guide for charities to company giving. I knew that it would be wanted, but at that stage I had no idea as to how I would get the information. I did find a way of doing that, and the book became the first in a growing series of grant directories which have all been updated every two or three years over the past 25 years, and the information has now been put online as well for people to subscribe to. This good idea became the cornerstone of a million-pound publishing operation.

4. **Start with the market and work backwards**. What do people want that relates to what you want to do? How can you provide it? What networks and distribution systems can you work with? One of the programmes I co-founded is UnLtd, the foundation which makes cash awards to emerging social entrepreneurs for them to turn their ideas into projects. When assessing applications I found that we had so many people with an idea for a product (e.g. reading books for dyslexic children or a campaign to beat bullying). Most were so enthused about their idea and wanted to produce a publication or a website that gave people good information but they had neglected to think about how people might access this information. I ran a series of workshops for them, including getting readers for your publication and getting visitors to your website, in order to get them to think about this. They all were able to come up with some good ideas which would make their idea more successful. And more recently, I met someone who has developed an innovative cooking stove which is carbon negative (that is, it returns more carbon to the environment than it burns). We came up with the idea of starting with outdoor barbecues, because these would be easier to sell than kitchen stoves and would not require changed behaviour or involve large installation costs. This would be a good point to start from, to get the technology understood and into people's homes.

5. **Take risks**. This is the essence of entrepreneurism. Have the
    confidence that yours is a good idea, and then do your utmost to
    make it work. Don't wait until you have everything neatly in place.
    That may never happen. The biggest risk I ever took was to launch
    an annual charity fair. I met someone and was talking about my idea,
    and he said that he had tried something like that and it didn't work.
    That was like a red rag to me. I wanted to prove that it could work.
    We hired an exhibition centre for four days, and the cost was greater
    than my organisation's reserves. So if it failed, the charity would go
    out of business. My trustees said that if I thought I could pull it off,
    I should do it. So I got started. And one of the nicest moments in
    my professional life was seeing the exhibitors putting up their stands
    on the day before the opening, then seeing the queues of people at
    the box office and meeting the hundred or so people who were
    running the workshops. We did a little better than break even: It
    was a success!

6. **Continue to innovate**. Your good idea is fresh and new, and that is
    what will propel you forward; but it needs refreshing, as otherwise
    it can become old and stale, and other people will be developing
    their own good ideas. I have set up a crowdfunding website to help
    people raise money for good causes. But so have a lot of other
    people. Ours is called Buzzbank, and is the only crowdfunding
    website that enables people to raise money through loans as well as
    donations, and which offers the possibility of backers having a share
    of the revenue from the projects that they are supporting. There is
    a lot of interest in what we are doing, but we need to do more than
    speak out at conferences and fairs. So alongside doing this, I am
    also trying to create some innovative ideas for how the website could
    be used, for example, for students to get the money they need to
    pay for their education, or to create online giving circles where
    people come together in their communities (it may be a school, a
    church or a neighbourhood) and together decide to support things
    that they jointly decide they want to make happen, or to link
    crowdfunding with start-up support, so that as well as getting the
    money, people assemble a crowd of people behind them who can
    cheer them on and provide other forms of support (including their
    time, their skills, their ideas and their contacts) which will help
    make the venture a success.

So these are some thoughts which I hope you will find useful. Think that you can do something, rather than you can't. Find a way of doing it. And then do it. I love the Nike slogan, "Just Do It".

❝ Fail to take that first step, and nothing will happen. ❞

Michael Norton

Director, Centre for Innovation in
Voluntary Action
www.civa.org.uk
www.click2change.com

Clear Returns

Dear would-be Entrepreneur,

SO MUCH ABOUT BUILDING A SUCCESSFUL start-up is about confidence and self-belief – you hear this all the time – but what about that little voice in your head that tells you "I'm just not up to this. I really don't know what I'm doing"?

The most useful lesson I have learned in starting up Clear Returns is that it is perfectly ok not to know everything. In fact, believing you know everything is probably going to do more harm than good. You'll be wrong and too deluded to even see it.

Becoming an entrepreneur, especially if you're in the CEO role, is a strange journey from specialist to generalist. Forget all the years you've spent becoming an expert in whatever it is you do, now your job is to find better experts than yourself and orchestrate some magic. First you have to woo these great people to work with you (probably for a ridiculously low initial reward, or as a free advisor) and then you have to keep wooing them to stay with you as you run headlong over distant mountains.

Make yourself official keeper of the thank you cards (I never go anywhere without an emergency thank you card in my bag). You may not be able to spread cash around (and you don't want to scatter equity too liberally) but you can express gratitude and kind thoughts where deserved.

The faster growing and more successful your start-up is, the less realistic is the option of going alone and doing everything by yourself. You need people around you who know more about their stuff than you do.

At the beginning especially, you'll find it strange that you spend less and less time doing your special thing you're really good at (in my case analytics) and more and more time doing stuff you suspect you are bordering on useless at (filling in forms, for example). You've got to soak up enough about all sorts of random stuff to get you by – and to help you identify those subject specialists you need to help you (particularly as informal advisors).

Get the perfectionist in you under control, good enough will just have to do – you're on a time and energy constraint. Books like *The Personal MBA* and *Accounting Demystified* have been a godsend to me, as have the Stanford Entrepreneurial Lectures on iTunes (it's great hearing that the CEO of Spotify or Dropbox has been wrestling with the same challenges you are going through right now). Being part of the start-up incubator at Entrepreneurial Spark has opened the door to critical external expertise; it's definitely worth considering locating your startup in a programme like this.

Don't beat yourself up about your knowledge gaps or personal weaknesses – instead, objectively identify those traits and use them to define the "job descriptions" of the people you'll need to surround yourself with. (These don't need to be employees or co-founders, they could be people you want on your advisory panel, or as personal mentors.) For example, I'm such a ridiculous optimist, I'd see opportunity in the apocalypse (just think of the sunset!) If I didn't balance that trait with more grounded, rational souls than me, we'd be on a one-way trip to the end of the world.

By understanding that it's OK to not know everything, you can turn it into a personal opportunity to always be learning. There's nothing wrong with "just in time" learning – and of course you can learn from your customers, your community and your peers, as well as through more formal channels. By pooling the skills of your advisors and team, you can only gain. Your business will be way more valuable if it's about more than just you. And you can foster that flexible, opportunity-focussed mindset that is so common in the best entrepreneurial businesses.

So, there is hope after all – not knowing everything is positively essential! It makes you listen to your customers and advisors, learn all the time, work hard, focus and stay flexible.

I hope that reassures anyone who was not feeling super-human this morning.

Best wishes,

Vicky Brock

CEO, Clear Returns
www.clearreturns.com

Dear Entrepreneur,

CUSKI BEGAN BACK IN '99 as a part-time venture by two working mums with the seed of an idea gleamed from their babies adopting items from around them and using them for comfort to sleep. Realising there was a gap in the market for a bespoke baby comforter, Cuski – which means 'To Sleep' in Welsh – was born.

The Cuski brand is now recognised and trusted all over the world, comforting 1000s of babies it has even been awarded the only NHS protocol ever given for a baby comforter in Europe.

There are now more Cuski products added to the range and the passion goes on.

Our personal strapline as we developed the Cuski brand was 'These Are The Good Times', which we still believe in and this keeps us motivated as it did during the harder times. Working in full-time jobs and struggling to keep Cuski afloat wasn't always easy. But we believed in our product and were prepared to make a lot of sacrifices, so in 2006 we gave up our jobs, sold our properties, moved into rented accommodation and got family and friends on board for child caring duties to enable us to raise enough cash. Cuski wasn't going to sell itself and we needed major awareness, editorials, trade shows, giveaways, awards under our belt, and most importantly more ORDERS.

Put your mind to it, it is achievable

Always remember, if you have a product you believe in then don't think national think international as we did – after all, babies are international and all have the same needs.

We successfully broke into the international market and our exports have steadily grown and grown and now make up the biggest part of our turnover, which it will for you too – I promise. Lots of new UK entrepreneurs we meet are daunted when they receive enquiries about their products from other countries, but we say you have got the enquiry, your product has raised interest so the rest is easy, just go for it, you have nothing to lose and everything to gain, so sell your product in as many countries as you possibly can. We found breaking into foreign markets to be one of the most rewarding and satisfying milestones of our journey.

I will give you one inspiring example of determination: many moons, and a couple of blue moons, ago we used to sell 24 Cuskis every six weeks to a distributor in a country far away. We would send them by surface mail which took six weeks to get there. This country has now grown to be our biggest consumer and these days they receive their orders by container loads direct from our factory.

Try and take five to recharge your batteries. Tiredness can lead to stress and your business won't move forward when you're out of sorts.

Think out of the box

Who wants to follow sheep? Be different and you will claim awareness. Make your work environment happy and inviting as you will be spending a lot of time there! Build relationships with your suppliers and your customers; they are equally important!

Be hot on social media. It's the most radical free advertising available so use it! A good percentage of our mail order business comes from Facebook. Give your customers an incentive to revisit, and make opening your package an uplifting experience. We use scented tissue paper, Cuski balloons, and include candy in each order.

Remember, referrals and recommendations are the finest accolade you will ever receive, so always use and work on these!

Don't give up when things go wrong as they invariably will do along the way. We have found these can sometimes be a blessing in disguise. Keep motivated and work your way through any obstacles that arise and, as we do, keep saying, "Those were and still are the good times"!

❝ Be hot on social media. It's the most radical free advertising available so use it! ❞

On a lighter note, you will always be an entertaining dinner guest!!

Key words: Determination, Gratitude, Dedication, Passion, Faith, Compassion, Gracious, Positivity, and last but not least, always Profitability.

Suzy & Judy

Founders, Cuski Baby Ltd
www.cuski.com

Karen Darby

I STARTED MY FIRST BUSINESS WHEN I WAS 22 years old and I very nearly didn't do it. I was afraid that I didn't know enough and that maybe I should wait until I had more experience. Then a friend and mentor said: 'Karen, sometimes you just have to grab the opportunity when it presents itself', and he was right. Several successful businesses on, I still don't know all the answers but I know one thing: the universe applauds action.

So my advice to you dear reader is to put this book down and just do it. Stop looking for answers and advice and hot tips from entrepreneurs, just take a gulp of breath and take the plunge. And if you are afraid, ask yourself: 'What's the worst that can happen and can I live with it?'

Karen Darby

www.karendarbydirect.com

Degree Art

Dear Entrepreneur,

WELCOME TO THE RIDE OF YOUR LIFE – nothing can beat the feeling of doing it for yourself. You are answerable only to yourself and now own your achievements as well as your failures!

Over the past ten years we have had so many experiences, all of which have made our business what it is today. There is much we didn't know or understand at the start of our journey, none of which would have altered our conviction and belief in our business' potential.

We have put down the key pieces of advice that have stuck with us along the way and which we continue to refer to.

FINANCIAL ADVICE

Know your numbers – It's your business and no one else can tell the figures for you so make sure you learn how to speak the language of finance even if it's not your thing.

Cash really is king (or queen) – Monitor your cash flow. Nothing kills a business faster than running out of cash.

Get your banking right – Know your bank manager and make sure they know you. This is a relationship worth pursuing.

Free money v earned money – Don't let the allure of pursuing sponsorship or grants prevent you from concentrating on earning money, which is the only way to build a sustainable business.

MARKETING

Consider yourself a brand – Don't feel shy about selling yourself as much as you do your business. You are at least half the reason people will buy into your idea.

Protect your ideas, don't hide them – Businesses that don't talk about what they do, fail. Ensure you safeguard by copyrighting, posting and keeping sealed copies of your business plan, patent if necessary, but don't hide it away from the world or it will simply fester whilst someone else succeeds in the space you have left vacant.

SURVIVING AS AN ENTREPRENEUR

Maintain a supportive community – It can get lonely so ensure you have support whether it be a business partner, family or friends who can give you a boost or lend a willing ear.

Understand that competition is healthy – It can be painful but know your competitors.

Select your mentors – Accept advice from mentors you chose and feel free to sack self-appointed or unhelpful advisors.

Network – It can be painful but is always surprisingly rewarding. Find the networks you enjoy.

Never be afraid to ask questions – better to ask than not to know.

PREPARING FOR GROWTH

Always be preparing for growth – Be organised and put systems in place from the outset. This will save you an unbelievable amount of time down the line.

Be prepared to do everything (at first) and then be prepared to let go later – You can't be an expert at it all but understand how things work so that you can be confident and knowledgeable. As you grow you can confidently outsource knowing you are freeing up your time to concentrate on your skilled areas.

Finally, never lose sight of your original destination or goals. **Be adaptable, brave and don't let the inevitable cynics knock your confidence.**

Good luck from us both.

Elinor and Isobel

Co-Founders, Degree Art Ltd
www.degreeart.com

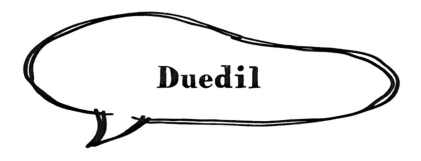

Duedil

Dear Entrepreneur,

Get experience

When I first started I didn't have a lot of experience. If I could go back I would gain experience by working as an intern. With the right experience I would have avoided a lot of mistakes.

Do what you know

By starting a business in a market you are familiar with you are a lot more prepared than you would be if you started in something you had no idea about.

The idea for my business came from my past career in risk assessment. I spotted a gap in the market and I went for it.

Work for yourself, but not yet

It is not a bad thing to work for someone else, not to begin with anyway. Before starting a business make sure you have the relevant experience and training in your field. The best type of training is in the workplace. Get a job with a company that does something similar and learn from their mistakes. This way you can make sure you are ready to start your own business. Too many people want to make a quick buck with zero experience.

You can start from scratch

Poverty is often an environment in which creativity can flourish. If you have nothing to lose then you might as well go for it, right? Constraints can make you look at things a different way.

Daily routines

- Keep meetings to days you know you won't be distracted.
- Give your staff freedom to work from home if they need to.
- Set times to check your email, e.g. twice a day or once an hour.
- Only write three sentence emails.

Persistence wins!

Ensure you can cope with rejection. It won't be an easy ride but as long as you stick it out you will become successful in business.

Good luck.

Damian Kimmelman
Founder, Duedil
www.duedil.com

Dear Entrepreneur,

FIRST OF ALL, CONGRATULATIONS on taking the time to read this book! Every great journey starts with a first step. By reading this book, you're taking a step forwards on the weird and wonderful journey of the entrepreneur. However, you must be warned in advance that this is no job for the faint hearted! It will take hard work, dedication, perseverance, and above all else passion, to see your 'creation' come alive! Read on, if you dare!

Opportunity identification

In every market, no matter if it is during a recession or boom time, there will be an opportunity for a new product or service to succeed. As an example, *The Economist* once wrote that when an economy is in growth, restaurants and cinemas will do extremely well, however in a recession companies such as Domino's Pizza and Netflix will do better as people 'downsize' their spending habits whilst maintaining a certain quality of life. The point here is that even in economic downturn there are companies growing faster than ever. Lesson here: there's no excuse to not set up a business anymore.

And if you think it's all been done before, you're wrong! As an example, new developments in technology give rise to new opportunities. Services on your phone that enable you to benefit from geo-targeted services (such as Foursquare, Poynt or Hailo) were inconceivable prior to the launch of GPS enabled handsets. The trick is being able to react quickly to the new opportunities that present themselves. Having a keen ear to the ground and finger on the pulse of the latest developments will go a long way towards getting you a first mover advantage.

Concept development

My previous experience working as a Strategy and New Venture Consultant helped me quite a bit in the early stages of developing the concept of my business. The experience taught me the importance of building a strong value proposition with a robust benefits case. What does this actually mean? In simple terms, it's about identifying a customer need or problem that can be serviced or solved by your product profitably (with an emphasis on the 'profit' part). Any idea you develop should be grounded in addressing a need in the market. Having said this, I constantly find myself surprised by companies who launch products that address a customer need that is somewhat more difficult to identify – such as giving your photos a retro 1970s feel using Instagram. The company, as we all know, was sold to Facebook in 2012 for the not so menial sum of $1bn. Although these make great front-page news stories, they are not the norm. Focus your concept development process on market fundamentals.

When I set up Eyetease in 2010, there was a clear trend towards migration of out-of-home media sites from print to digital – with digital out-of-home (DOOH) advertising spend growing at warp speed. Why? Two main reasons: greater revenue potential per site for media owners (c. 5 to 6 times multiplier on ad revenue generated from static media sites as they could now run multiple ads in a loop) and greater creative flexibility and impact for brands. One of the last of these out-of-home media formats to move to digital was the taxi (or taxi media) – a common feature of every city and, by their

> **❝ If you think it's all been done before, you're wrong! ❞**

very essence, always present wherever there are people. Upon first inspection it appeared to be a strange concept – merging digital signage with taxis seemed folly! But here began the intrigue. Imagine a world where taxi media could be updated remotely within seconds and play adverts to the right people, at the right place and at the right time. Imagine a world where there were no production costs or lead times – two very real problems currently experienced with taxi vinyl advertising in the UK. Could taxis generate the same 5 to 6 times multiplier on ad revenue by becoming digital? A further deep dive uncovered trials of a similar proposition in the US by a leading media company back in 2006 – later discontinued due to the technology being unreliable. It was clear from the research that the concept and value proposition to both media owners and brands were excellent, but the technology needed to be robust and reliable to succeed. And so the iTaxitop was born.

Launch

Developing the iTaxitop was no easy task. The fact we were the only company trying to make this made the task seem harder but also much more worthwhile! No job will ever prepare you for life as an entrepreneur. Developing a radically new concept was not without its challenges. I spent over two years developing the iTaxitop, which as a pre-revenue business can be immensely crippling. When there's no easy way to develop something new you have to start from the beginning and work your way up. Funding was always an issue and certainly presented a real hurdle to progress in the early stages. What ever you think it'll cost to make, multiply it by five and you might get close to the number you'll eventually spend. I operated a stage-and-gate process to investment with every key milestone market validation matched by a round of funding. It wasn't easy and certainly required a lot of sacrifices to see the dream become a reality. From renting out my bedroom and sleeping on a blow-up bed for three months to help fund the build of our first website, all the way to endless hours/days/months in the cold testing the prototype, was far from glamorous!

What I would say is that my passion and belief in the product pulled me through the tough times. And not to forget, I implore you to not start a business without a strong support network throughout the process. My amazing parents, sister and girlfriend helped me through the low points and celebrated with me the high points. That's not to say they all believed in the concept, but they believed in me as a person who could

> **66 What ever you think it'll cost to make, multiply it by five and you might get close to the number you'll eventually spend. 99**

make this happen. Having people like this close to you is as important – if not more – than having all the money in the world.

As a final thought, here's my top five do's and don'ts when launching a new product, which I hope will expedite your learning curve and growth cycle when launching your business:

1. **Understand the value of money.** This is key. When launching a business, you soon realise there is not an infinite supply of cash at your disposal – every penny must count. It's about considering every decision with several different lenses and perspectives.

2. **Think strategically.** When developing a new concept, think objectively, do your research and be clear on where you make money. Adopt a stage-and-gate process to funding, whereby for every validation in your product/service, you invest more. Set these checkpoints early on and make sure you keep to them!

3. **Simplicity is key.** Get your value proposition and benefits case right from the beginning! If you can't sell it in one sentence, move on! If you can't identify a clear benefit to a clear customer group, move on!

4. **Get tough but listen closely.** Be prepared for rejection and criticism from outsiders. Most of it will be based on reasons that are either skewed by a conflicting agenda, an underdeveloped knowledge of your product or you're simply not selling the proposition right! However, some of the best advice I received was from some of the most sceptical of audiences. Listen closely and think objectively. Take a step back and provoke yourself to consider your product as someone else's – you might be interested to see the results. Thinking differently early on in the process (with different lenses) will help you evolve your proposition and enable you to address concerns and

exploit benefits directly with your customer! This will help ensure you give customers a compelling, and truly awesome, pitch – so listen closely to all those naysayers!

5. **Get your name out there and be seen!** Spend time using social media – 'tweet about it'! Attend networking events and follow up with contacts. Find people on LinkedIn and get a meeting. Write press releases, send them out! Apply to awards, be a member, attend networking events…if they can't see you, they can't buy from you!

Today, Eyetease is ranked in the top 100 startups and top 20 up-and-coming tech companies in the UK. We are the only company globally to have successfully manufactured a ruggedised broadcast media solution for taxis, and following three months of technical certification and approvals, Eyetease signed up as an approved supplier to the world's largest taxi media company. With trials in several major US and UK cities underway, the iTaxitop is set to become a common feature of the urban landscape and a game changing communication tool for brands, media owners and the public to enjoy for years to come!

And if you're still not inspired to start something new, remember this: If you try something new, you risk failure. If you don't try something new, you're guaranteed failure. So try it today!

Yours faithfully,

Richard Corbett

Founder and CEO, Eyetease
www.eyeteasemedia.com

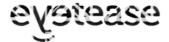

FaceFlow

Dear Entrepreneur,

Your life – your book.

I was a college student of 20 years old, I knew nothing about programming and two years later, I owned a website with over half a million members and living my life from it – and it's just the beginning. I am not close to where I want to be yet. It's not easy to fully plunge into a new passionate project you may have when you are living a stable life. To me, that is exactly one of the reasons why I did not continue my formal education – I would rather have an exciting life of ups and downs, of failures and successes, of struggles and comfort, than the stable 9-5 lifestyle of 99% of the people. I believe our purpose in life is about trying out stuff, working hard and being obsessed about what you care about and your goals. You must get in the mud of life in order to get to the higher ground.

In a world where information is rapidly shared and easily available, you can learn anything you set your mind to, as long as you stay motivated and dedicated toward your goals. If you think you are lacking knowledge in the areas you would like to do business in, you no longer need to sit for years behind a school desk, you can now learn and progress at a very fast pace.

The best thing to do is to get started while keeping your job or staying at school. That's what I did while I was in school – I had a vision and even though I had no idea how to go about it, I started learning and talking to programmers, I was learning a lot of new stuff every day and after a few weeks, I had my first prototype for my website. It didn't cost me a lot – I was using my savings from my previous summer job (instead of buying a car or getting drunk like many students would do, remember: sacrifices) and this first prototype allowed me to get to know a little about a lot of things. The next version of my website was much better as I learned from my mistakes and I am not the type of guy who makes the same mistakes twice. After the next summer, I used most of my savings again, and we could get something built that would be much better, and it never stopped progressing. I stopped school when I knew I could make a living out of being an entrepreneur. Even though I am still struggling in my journey, so far life has been much better and I envision the rest of my life to be that way too.

Dany Pelletier

Founder, FaceFlow
www.faceflow.com

Flamingo

Dear Entrepreneur,

HERE ARE A FEW LITTLE GEMS I've learnt from ten years in entrepreneurship. I hope they are useful!

You are never too young

I started my business at 22 and have never looked back. In fact, ten years on, I think it's easier to begin your business when you are younger – you're more willing to take risks and you're not tied down with responsibilities and other commitments. There is nothing holding you back from achieving your dreams, whatever your age!

Become a trustee

Being a trustee for a local charity is a great way to get involved in your local community, to make a contribution and to learn new skills – particularly those relating to leadership, governance and decision-making. An incredibly low number of young people are trustees and even fewer realise it is possible to take up such positions. Many charities and non-profits are crying out for new trustees and love to see new, younger faces on board.

Never burn a bridge

No matter how someone behaves or how much they upset you, always be polite and keep your cool. You never know when your paths may cross again and you might need their skills or contacts, or vice versa.

Contribute to the community

I believe we all have a responsibility to be active corporate citizens. And businesses who do good also tend to do well. Getting involved with community groups and charities is a great way to make contacts and get yourself known. It's win-win.

Challenge yourself

Outside of work, step out of your comfort zone once in a while. Jump out of a plane, go wild swimming, do something you're afraid of. You'll be surprised how strong you are and you can draw on that experience at later points.

Radiators not drains

Gather positive, can-do people around you who have the skills to do what you can't – and focus on your gift. Avoid those who belittle your dreams.

Bloom where you're planted

You can't always control who you're working for or what you're doing. But you can control the experience whilst you're there.

The sun doesn't shine forever

When things are going well, it's all too easy to sit back and enjoy the ride. However, this is the time to prepare for a downturn. Thinking ahead and being prepared can save a business when bad times hit.

The harder you work the luckier you get

There's no substitute for good old-fashioned hard work, it really does pay off.

Inspire yourself

Travel, read, try new things. Put yourself in other people's shoes. All essential to keep fresh ideas coming!

Look after yourself

Keeping fit and healthy really is important, especially when you work long hours and are under extreme pressures. Get up an hour earlier and go for a swim, cycle to work or run home. Find an activity that works for you. Exercise is amazing for clearing your head and you'll be surprised how much a blast of fresh air and some physical exertion will make the ideas flow – you'll get twice as much done.

Adapt and evolve

Be aware of what's going on around you, be quick to evolve and keep things fresh. Make sure your business has a flexible, simple structure to enable you to respond and adapt quickly and easily.

Good luck!

Katie Sparkes
Founder, Flamingo
www.flamingo-creative.co.uk

Bollocks To That!

Entrepreneurial advice from Jon Allen, founder of rugby fashion brand, Front Up

Dear Entrepreneur,

As a budding entrepreneur you will no doubt be busy planning your future world domination so I will keep this short and sweet for you.

You can make it happen

Front Up Rugby began life in a one-bedroom flat in Coventry. I had little money and no knowledge of the clothing industry.

What I did have was a business concept I had researched and believed in and that I knew there was a gap in the market for. I was convinced I could create a brand with a strong enough DNA and identity to thrive.

What I also had was myself and tremendous support from my wife and family.

All entrepreneurs share a certain set of characteristics that enable their business ideas to thrive. You could have the best idea in the world but without an entrepreneur behind it, it is far less likely to succeed.

It is YOU that makes things happen and finds a way forward when the chips are down. You have to be creative, intuitive, determined, focused, passionate and have an unfloundering belief in yourself and desire to succeed. One of the main differences that separate entrepreneurs is their gut instinct. Following your gut instinct is a powerful tool and sometimes very hard to do. But it is this innate characteristic that enables some to succeed and others to fail. No-one understood what I was trying to achieve with Front Up. It was only my gut instinct that said I could make it happen.

It's not meant to be easy, otherwise everyone would succeed at it. It's down to the little margins, the extra energy when you're tired, making that last phone call, finding a way to convert a no to a yes and not giving up at the first (second or third…) hurdle.

It takes 100% commitment and you need to find a way to enjoy the challenge and keep focused on your goals.

Not everyone will agree with you….many will think you're crazy and others will advise you to perhaps 'look at other things'. Bollocks to that. Crack on, prove them wrong, turn this into positive energy; use what makes you, you.

What if it fails? What if I make myself look stupid? So what? Never die not knowing. Follow your dreams. If you do fail (and as an entrepreneur I will assume you will not take this option lightly), so what? You've stood up, got out there, tried to make it happen, learnt a hell of a lot and become a better person along the way.

You learn more from your mistakes than anything else. The key is not to make them again and use these experiences positively in the future; which is easier said than done. No-one knows all the answers straightaway, it's how you develop along the journey that counts.

Endless entrepreneurs fail initially, but dust themselves off and find a way to succeed in the end. Simon Cowell, Richard Branson and numerous others have all been at the bottom of the pile, scrapping around trying to make it happen. The key is THEY FOUND A WAY.

I don't believe in luck. The more you try the more luck you will get (in the end). 'Luck' rewards effort, perseverance and dedication. Some would say I was 'lucky' when we won our first contract with Debenhams or when I found investors for the business on LinkedIn. No, I went out and made these things happen – and it's a bloody great feeling when you pull it off, as it will often be against the odds.

Take the challenge. It won't be easy. Celebrate the small wins along the way, believe in your vision and yourself, stay focused, ignore the naysayers and 'Good Luck'.

Jon Allen

Founder, Front Up Rugby

www.frontup.co.uk

FRONT UP
RUGBY
GUTS & GLORY

The Giving Card

Write a business plan. Then rip it up.

IT'S ALWAYS A GOOD IDEA TO HAVE a general direction for your business to go in, but no two days are ever the same. Your initial concepts and beliefs about how your company will launch and operate will probably change more frequently than the British weather! No matter how much preparation you do, it is inevitable that unpredictable obstacles will be thrown your way. The only thing you can do is prepare for these difficulties by attempting to predict as many eventualities as possible and potential solutions to combat each one. That's where a business plan does come in handy. If it's just you in the company, write yourself a to-do list each morning and follow it; it will give you the direction you need each day. If you've got a team (which I strongly recommend), have daily meetings with everyone – just take five minutes out to hear their agendas and set targets based on what's important to the business today. (If you do decide to rip up your business plan, make sure you've kept a digital copy just in case...!)

Ask people if they like your idea until you find someone who says no

When was the last time you told someone they didn't look good when they asked? People are usually very complimentary and supportive when you ask them for their opinion, but how do you find out what people really think? Ask someone to actually buy into your idea and see what they say. It's just as important to understand why people don't like something so you can address it. Speak to your potential clientele (the ones who will actually pay for your product or service) and see if they would invest, and if not, why not? By tailoring the business to your clienteles exact needs (instead of guessing their requirements) you can develop a business, be it a product or service that is highly sought-after. Secondly, by involving your future clientele as much as possible in the early stage design process, it is almost like a tailored product for each customer. However it must be remembered that you cannot please everyone if it is not in the best interests of your business.

Build a team: don't think you can do it all yourself

Once you've come up with the idea, it seems like you're ready to go. You can bring in expertise at a cost, but how do you know they're any good? You need specialists in a number of different areas to make a business function. I've often thought I can do it all myself, but you quickly learn that you can't be afraid to delegate, or ask for help. Make a list of your strengths and weaknesses and see where you need to fill in the gaps. You don't have to start forking out lots of money; look to friends and family who will often have very different skills to you and may be willing to offer their time for free.

Work on turning yourself into a brand. Russell and Jo did it.

People will often buy into the businessperson and not just the merchandise, whether this is an investor or a consumer. It was with this lesson that I developed a passion for business and recognised the importance of being a 'face' for your company and not just someone who sits sending emails all day. People really do invest in the individual. If you are trusted, respected and have a reputation to deliver, people will want to work with you. Don't tell people your business 'will do'; tell them 'it does'. Always talk about your business in a positive light; confidence is infectious.

Don't set a completion date for building a website. It will never be finished.

The internet is evolving daily and you'll always want to keep up-to-date. Despite thorough planning, there will always be improvements that need to be made based on what your users/customers say. Make sure you factor these in to your financial projections for website design and development; there is the initial building, but then the maintenance of the site too. Also bear in mind that domain names cost year-on-year as does the website hosting; these small costs quickly mount up.

Pitch and putt them in their place...

It's all very well going to networking events, but make sure you have your '30-second pitch' prepared. When someone asks (which they inevitably will) 'what is it you do?', you are prepared with a natural sounding, confident pitch about your business. Also try and fit in who you are looking to meet as they will probably be able to refer you to someone else nearby, or a colleague. Try and end your 'pitch' with a question about them; find out who they are, what they do and if they can help you. If you can ask them what they do first, before they have a chance, you're onto a winner. It means you can quickly decide if they can help and how to tailor your pitch.

Keep your enemies close, but your contact book closer

Keep a business card file or else you'll end up losing lots of contacts!

Be sure to take every opportunity to speak in public about you or your business – it's a great way of people learning more about what you're capable of. Even if public speaking isn't your thing, a great way to practice is by interacting with like-minded people at business networking events. Search online for ones which are near, relevant and fit in with your timetable; some are before work, during the day and others are in the evening or at the weekend. The contacts you make here will be invaluable.

Dan Taylor

The Giving Card
www.thegivingcard.co.uk

Gnewt Cargo

G NEWT CARGO WAS A LABOUR OF LOVE, from 18 months before we even opened the doors until today, two and a half years later. The road has certainly not been easy, it has been very challenging, but it has also been extremely stimulating and rewarding. Why go through life without a challenge, after all that is why you're considering being an entrepreneur right?! We have grown Gnewt Cargo steadily from a standing start and with no practical knowledge of the logistics industry. Lots of things have conspired to get us to where we are today, and we are by no means finished or think we have achieved what we set out to do. There is plenty of work still to do but we have learned a few things and we hope to share them with you here.

People will often tell you to only start a business in something that you know a lot about, and that you are passionate about. This is true. However, in some cases not knowing what you're letting yourself into can be a blessing otherwise you perhaps wouldn't have ever gone into it knowing what was around the corner! Let me explain. I now have no hair. This could be due to my mother and father's recessive genes being passed down to me, but it is also probably due in part to the immense pressure of starting and running a business. I don't mean to be the harbinger of doom(!) but it is sensible to make prospective entrepreneurs aware that it's not plain sailing, otherwise everyone would do it. You're not guaranteed success, you're not guaranteed those 20 days holiday, you're not guaranteed the monthly pay cheque. You are, however, guaranteed a vast learning experience, far greater than if you were to work for someone else. The fact that we essentially threw ourselves in at the deep end to start this business with no prior knowledge was a blessing as it made us even more determined to make it work and provided a launchpad from which our learning curve went stratospheric. We have learnt quickly and adapted even quicker.

We have fostered very good relationships. These relationships are with our employees as well as with our clients and contacts in the industry. Good contacts and especially contacts that have been nurtured over time (never just take from a contact, it is always a two-way street) have enabled us to get our name out in the ether and have thus enabled us to build our brand, gain credibility in the industry and grow. Client relationships are very important. Knowing when to pick your battles over price or to let something go is a key skill when it comes to managing your relationship with your clients. Good engagement and contact with clients is essential – that doesn't necessarily mean calling them up every single day but it does mean getting to know them and what makes them tick and trying to understand deeply how in their view you are faring for them. Perhaps it is even just occasionally sending them an article that might be of relevance to them to let them know you are thinking of them. Every little helps. A good relationship with staff is ultimately what will make or break your business. I mean this in a couple of ways. One is having the ability to pick the right soldiers who you want to come on the journey with you. A fish rots from the head so in order to get your culture right within your workplace you must give key roles to those who buy into your philosophy and vision otherwise this will be ever harder to filter through to the rest of the team. If you have a few people leading and singing off the same hymn sheet it becomes a lot easier. Another way I mean having good relationships with staff is through treating them well. Obvious right?! No. Humans are complex and as your business grows, managing people gets harder, so get this right early on. Constantly remind them of how they fit into the organisation, of how they are doing, train them well and give them the occasional Friday beers or small gesture to show them that they are appreciated. I once hand wrote individual messages to all the staff telling them why I wanted them on my team during this journey – it went down very well and they haven't forgotten it.

> **" Knowing when to pick your battles over price or to let something go is a key skill when it comes to managing your relationship with your clients. "**

A third key point that I encourage you to take heed of, and I am only starting to put this into practice myself, is to try to focus on things that only you can do. This is easier said than done because when you start up you need to be involved in everything, but once you manage to get some scale, try to hand over tasks and processes that enable you to lift your head from the minutiae and concentrate on what you do best. It may well be that you are good at marketing, or strategy, or both, but if that is where you add most value, concentrate on it and delegate or outsource those things you can afford to. If you use your time well, it is here that you will build the most value most quickly in your business.

Matthew Linnecar

Founder & Director,
Gnewt Cargo
www.gnewtcargo.co.uk

Gourmet Origins

Dear Entrepreneur,

What would you advise yourself if you could go back to the day you started your business?

I would start a lot more focused. At the very beginning of the project we tried to do many things at the same time and this ended up in delays in those parts of the project that were very relevant. Sometimes you might find out what is relevant – or not – as you go, but in any case I would start by focusing on something first and taking the project from there.

What inspired you to start a business?

I had always wanted to start something on my own, it was just the circumstances, like not having found an ideal partner before, and, let's admit it, a bit of fear to sail alone, that had deterred me from doing it. I think the ability to develop your own ideas is a very powerful driver.

Is it possible to start from scratch?

Absolutely, if you are willing to go through the hardships that working with little resources entail. This is something that can be particularly daunting for those that are used to working in a corporate environment with security and perks. It is not for everyone, but being lean allows you to make mistakes and grow at your own pace.

How we built our brand and developed our idea

The current GourmetOrigins.com marketplace was not exactly our original idea, it's the result of multiple trial and error experiments, even our business model was different, but I think in this case, having good mentors, such as our seed investors Openfund, helped us shape our business idea and develop it accordingly. The current GourmetOrigins.com is a lot more focused. We do not intend to do everything for everyone. We were not happy with the online platforms for foodies that were in the market; most of them concentrated on cooking and recipes whereas we wished to focus on the traceability and ingredients. We wanted to tell the food's "story". We started as an information-based website, but soon we realised it would be a much more useful and powerful proposition if we allowed people to shop for the sort of unique products we display. We also wanted it to be an international platform from day one, despite being aware of the difficulties this can entail in Europe where things like logistics and banks normally work along national markets. We had to have lots of patience sorting this sort of "logistical" issue but we think we can provide additional value, precisely by breaking these barriers for our consumers. Here we are, and we expect to continue developing our concept further in the near future!

Miquel Ross

Founder, Gourmet Origins
www.gourmetorigins.com

Humanima CIC

Passion, Patience and Persistence

Having seen many people miserable in their 9-5 jobs, I have always been a firm believer that if you are going to work for three quarters of your life, then it may as well be doing something that you love. I've heard all manner of excuses from people saying that they couldn't do what they love because they don't know how, they haven't got the time, they haven't got the money or they don't know if it would work, bla bla bla! Nobody said that starting a business would be easy, but from the outset you need to keep reminding yourself **why** you are doing it.

HumAnima CIC came about as a result of a lifelong passion for the human-animal bond. It is that passion that has kept me going for the two plus years of establishing the business (without payment) and that has helped me to keep my focus on my goal of creating a career that I love and that will have a positive impact on those I work with – furry and not so furry!

I have created HumAnima CIC because I love working with people and I love animals. I didn't know how to combine my love of both into a career that would allow me to work with both animals and humans in a meaningful and productive way and there certainly were not any careers that you could simply train for which did just that, so I created my own. It was neither simple nor straightforward, especially as one cannot be an "Animal Assisted Therapist". By the Delta Society's definition, Animal Assisted Therapy (AAT) "is directed and/or delivered by a health/human service professional with specialised expertise, and within the scope of practice of his/her profession." Therefore I needed a health profession within which I could specialise as an AAT professional – for me, that was counselling.

Partly, all this has come about as a result of melding my many interests but more than anything it has been because I believed in the concept I was creating, and the passion I have for my interests is what drove me consistently to keep moving forward. If you have an interest that you love passionately, whether it's mountain biking, gardening, reading or knitting, you have the potential to create something – push your passion to enterprise. If you are willing to think outside the box, be creative and flexible there will always be an opportunity that utilises your knowledge and interests with a productive result. I've had some whacky ideas in the past but if you don't take the risk you will never, ever know, and the only one to blame will be yourself. As the saying goes, "Playing life as the safe option is possibly the riskiest thing you could do", and this links in nicely with my own motto, "Strive to live life without regrets", as none of us know if this is really the only shot we'll get so make the most of it.

As I've already said, it's been two (plus) long years of part-time pushing at my ideas and giving them structure and form. This could not have been done without patience. Lots of it. Something **66 Push your passion to enterprise. 99** that I have found to help develop my own patience was mindful meditation. Lots of it. A lot of people consider it to be "fluffy" but that could not be further from the truth. This has been a particularly useful skill to develop especially as it helps to develop focus and attention.

Finally, persistence. Otherwise known as determination. Willpower. Resolve. Purpose. Whatever you want to call it. Your passion is your fire

❝ With your passion, patience and persistence anything is possible! ❞

that will drive your determination. Use it to its full advantage because you will get tired, you will have low points, you will think of giving up. Do not expect other people to give you that much needed pep-talk that will help you get your mojo back. It is ultimately down to you and your belief in your ideas and, as fluffy as it may sound, making your dreams come true. Everyone can make their dreams come true, regardless of what that dream is. Honestly. But only you can give yourself permission to let that dream sprout, grow and develop. You have to nurture it and look after it the same as you would care for any living organism. You will not only be your own boss but you are your own responsibility, and that is perhaps the hardest part. If you keep making excuses to other people for whatever reason, it is actually yourself you are letting down. However, with your passion, patience and persistence anything is possible!

Kathryn Kimbley, MSc (MBACP)

Founder,
HumAnima CIC
www.humanima.co.uk

Innocent

Dear Entrepreneur,

IN 1999 I STARTED A SMOOTHIE COMPANY called innocent with my two best friends, Jon and Adam. Thirteen years later, we are the number one smoothie brand in the UK (and across Europe) and each week we sell more than 2 million smoothies, turning over more than £200 million each year.

Over the years we've discovered a great deal about starting and running a business, having ideas and thinking differently, building a brand from nothing, and which fruits taste nicest together. We think our ideas are pretty universal. They could apply to any business, and we've got a few here to share with you (we'll probably leave out the fruit-based ones – you can look in our recipe book for the best smoothie combinations if you're interested).

We'd wanted to set up a business together for ages and one day decided to get on with it. So we began thinking about areas where we could identify a problem, and then how we'd solve it. Our first idea was The Amazing Electric Bath. It was going to be brilliant. Until its one small, but insurmountable, flaw dawned on us – having water and electricity in such close proximity to each other wasn't the greatest idea after all.

After that, we thought about what we'd like to buy but couldn't. We realised there were lots of people, just like us, who wanted to be healthy but found that it wasn't actually that easy when you're young and busy and rushing around all day. Pretty soon we hit upon the idea of natural fruit smoothies.

There was already a brand called PJs selling bottled smoothies in the UK, which was a good thing as it meant a market for smoothies definitely existed, but also presented us with the challenge of how to make ours better than theirs. One of our most used phrases is **always keep the main thing the main thing**. This means to understand why you're different and not let that slip – our main thing has always been that we would make our drinks the natural way. PJs used concentrates, which may have been easier and more profitable, but ultimately meant a compromise on taste and nutritional quality. Every decision we made back then, and make now, is based around keeping the main thing the main thing.

Once you've got your idea, it's important to actually begin. We've been pitched enough businesses in our time to know that most people have an idea for a business. But the majority don't even begin working on the opportunity, mainly because the whole project seems so intimidating. Basically, it's hard to see how you're going to build yourself a global multi-billion-dollar business when you're sat in your kitchen nibbling on a biscuit.

But the cliché is true: every business in the world started small. M&S began life as a market stall and YouTube was started by two friends in a room above a pizza takeaway. Even in today's heavily competitive world, little can still get big. So my advice is simple: **start small, but do get started**. There's nothing like taking the first small step to help get you over the initial fear and inertia that surrounds creating your own venture. Once you've committed to action, you'll find momentum comes from the pitter-patter of those first baby steps.

> **❝ It's hard to see how you're going to build yourself a global multi-billion-dollar business when you're sat in your kitchen nibbling on a biscuit. ❞**

We continue to 'start small' with any new initiative we embark upon, be it establishing ourselves in a new country, launching a new product, or testing out a new marketing campaign. It allows us to be more entrepreneurial – we can test ideas quickly and without breaking the bank. And then if we see potential, we put serious money behind the initiative to accelerate growth and make the most of the opportunity.

Once you've started, it's important to make sure everyone's in the same boat and has a **sense of purpose**. Right from the beginning of innocent, we were clear about one thing: we wanted to make it easy for people to do themselves some good – and set up a company we could be proud of. This purpose has helped us create five innocent values that we use all the time. A few years ago, we sat everyone down and asked them their ideas on what innocent was for and against. One version had us being against guns and pro-cheese. Certainly true, but not so relevant on a day-to-day basis. Collectively, we decided that our values are to be: responsible, entrepreneurial, generous, commercial and natural.

We now use our values as a filter when recruiting people (if they don't personally resonate with our values, they're not going to get the best out of innocent and we're not going to get the best out of them). We develop people in line with our values, and we reward people living them. In short, we take them seriously.

So we had our idea for what innocent would be and stand for, and we were desperate to get going. We then quickly realised that **everything takes longer than you think**. It may seem obvious but it's so easy to get over-optimistic and carried away thinking that things will happen instantly. More often than not, they don't. Whatever length of time you think it's going to take, triple it, and then add some more. We gave ourselves one month to get innocent up and running, and it took us nine – and as a result our finances were pretty tight. Looking back, I'd recommended staying in your existing job for as long as you can. Not only do you retain a source of income, but assuming you don't take the mickey too much, a workplace can provide resources, contacts, opportunities for market research and most, importantly, free sandwiches and coffee. It may mean working yourself to the bone, but there are many business ventures that never got off the ground purely because the founders could no longer support themselves.

66 Whatever length of time you think it's going to take, triple it, and then add some more. 99

Finally, I would say that it's important to **listen**. Businesses that don't listen end up failing. In order to gather information from the people that will make your business work, you need to stay in touch and put out as many feelers and sensors as you can. Everything you do should suggest an attitude of availability and a willingness to listen. Each and every method is valuable, even the less engaging and more traditional ones, because taken together they give you access to the minds of the people that are buying your product.

66 Businesses that don't listen end up failing. 99

Fundamentally, no matter how tough it's been, no matter how many times we've been told 'no' or 'it won't work', not for one second has any of us regretted the moment we set up innocent full time. If you're thinking of setting up your own business, we couldn't recommend it highly enough.

Good luck,

Richard Reed

Co-founder, Innocent Drinks Limited
www.innocentdrinks.co.uk

 **innocent**

Insider Trends

Dear Entrepreneur,

HERE ARE SOME OF THE MOST IMPORTANT TIPS I would have loved to have heard when I began my business.

Read

Buy, beg or borrow every business book you think you might like to read – you'll gain skills worth thousands, if not millions. Here are some of the ones I couldn't live without: *The E-Myth Revisited, HBR's 10 Must Reads on Strategy, The 4 Hour Workweek* and *Get to the Top on Google*. Also gain access to the LinkedInfluence online course – it will transform your business or you get your money back. I'm not sponsored to say any of this, by the way!

Experiment

Research and planning are vital, but experiments give the most accurate insights of all. Run as many experiments as you can afford, in all aspects of your business. Measure results, keep the ideas that work and modify whatever doesn't. Some things won't work at all – don't fret it, chuck them out and congratulate yourself on finding this out so quickly. Experiments make you move forward faster, partly because you'll launch things faster, and also because you'll gain the insight needed to perfect them faster.

Find out what works, and do it over and over again

One of the best pieces of advice I've ever been given. It relates to the 80/20 rule, or the Pareto principle, which states that 80% of your business will come from 20% of your clients, 80% of your profits will come from 20% of your turnover, 80% of your exposure will come from 20% of your marketing activity, and so on. After running a number of different experiments, sit down and look at the numbers – you'll see the 80/20 pattern popping up in all aspects of your business. You'll probably discover that you have one or two breakthrough products and services and one or two key ways that your biggest clients find out about you, all hidden in a raft of offerings and marketing tactics. Once you've identified these 80% centres, work out how you can focus more of your team's and customers' attention on them to accelerate your success.

Focus on profit, not turnover

It's easy to think that a lot of activity leads to success. In reality, a high level of activity, when spread too thinly, prevents success. Turnover comes from creativity and activity, but profit comes from efficiency and repetition. And at the end of the day, profit's the only financial figure that matters. As a creative entrepreneur, it takes a huge amount of discipline to value repetition, but it's essential to achieving success without burning out.

Suck it up

Setting up a business is hard work – it's basically two full-time jobs for one person during the first few years. And it's stressful – difficult times will always follow good, that's the nature of a growing or changing business. It takes a long time, too – an average of seven years for a business to become truly sustainable. The trick is to accept that these things are part and parcel of entrepreneurship, rather than assuming it has anything to do with your performance. If you can accept these things, you'll have more emotional energy to put into building your business, rather than wasting it trying to fight inescapable truths. Suck it up.

Believe in yourself and your idea – I wish you the best of luck!

Cate Trotter

Founder, Insider Trends Ltd
www.insider-trends.com

Junior's Pantry

Dear Entrepreneur,

So HAS THE LIGHT BULB GONE OFF or has it been an idea slowly cooking in your brain for months or even years? For me it was a light bulb moment pure and simple. I hadn't intended to ever start my own business, I had worked in the City for years and had always thought that this would be what I would do, although I hadn't been very happy for several years.

I was lucky I got the opportunity to move on and I thought I would be a stay-at-home mother for the first time (see I'm not a typical entrepreneur, I'm over 40, have children, live in the countryside – not the young thrusting type you might expect!) But it was exactly this experience of being at home that gave me the idea for my business. I was cooking a lot for my children and then for my husband, and I realised there weren't any healthy balanced meals for children (plenty for toddlers) in the supermarkets so I decided to create one and hey presto, Junior's Pantry was born.

I suppose this is one of the key lessons to being an entrepreneur; get involved in something you understand, something you love, something you want, something you need, as this will help you at every turn. I could have had the best idea for a widget to stop airplanes using too much fuel but as

I know nothing about widgets, airplanes or fuel it would have been a massive learning process and a huge uphill battle. As it is, I have cooked professionally, so know a bit about food (but nothing about mass production) and I have children, and know lots of children, so at least I was in an area I was familiar with.

> **❝ Get involved in something you understand, something you love, something you want, something you need, as this will help you at every turn. ❞**

My start point was to prove there was a gap in the market and that there would be a need. I used resources like the British Library for sector research and my local library had a good selection of business books. It also had other resources, for example I wasn't prepared to initially buy a subscription to industry magazine *The Grocer*, but the library had a copy I was able to borrow.

I ran research amongst a group of mums I knew (who didn't know that it was my idea, I told them I was helping someone out with market research). They spread this as a viral email far and wide – again another advantage of doing something you have an infinity with; I can access large groups of mothers with children under ten but I couldn't possibly get hold of that many 18 to 21 year olds for example. Once I was committed to the business and could see that I had a future with Junior's Pantry I gained in confidence.

My key bits of advice would be the following:

- **If you need help, ask.** Try friends, ex colleagues, family members, you never know who might know someone, who knows someone who could be helpful to you.

- **Make lists and/or a project plan.** My husband runs his own business and was very good at poking holes in what I was doing and challenging me. I knew where I wanted to get to, but wasn't always totally clear on how I would get there. He made me make a big project plan on Excel (like a revision timetable with colour – it took me ages!) with a countdown to a fictitious launch date (which actually turned out to only be a week out from our actual launch). On it was listed everything I had to do week by week – conversations with Trading Standards, ordering pots, talking to printers, getting the website created, etc. It didn't all get done when it should have but it kept me focused.

- **Expect it to be a lonely business**, I was on my own and that was particularly tough. At times it's great as you can make decisions quickly without long debates over pretty small details like the shade of yellow on the packaging. I was pleased to start the business on my own, it was my idea, my baby and I felt strongly it was mine to either succeed with or screw up and it was great to not have a responsibility to anyone else in the early days. The flip side of this is obviously there is no one to share the tough bits with and the burden can become very hard – I felt physically ill in the week running up to launch as there was so much to do.

- And lastly, **it is a rollercoaster** – the highs and lows are huge (I had seen this first-hand from my husband but experiencing it is something else), elation to depression in minutes! Also, if you are physically launching something expect to feel a bit low after the event – so much work has gone into the launch and if it all goes well (which it should if you've worked hard) you can feel a bit bereft afterwards and it takes a bit of time to get your mojo back into gear and push on to the next phase.

Launching Junior's Pantry is without a shadow of a doubt the best thing I've ever done – I have never felt so alive, so in control of my life and so content with what I've achieved in such a short space of time.

It is going to be a rollercoaster, but worth it. I believe life is for living, not watching from the sidelines. If you're questioning whether you should do it, just ask yourself, how would you feel if you saw or heard that someone had done what you were planning? If that thought causes you pain (as it did me), stop reading now and get on with it!!

Best wishes,

Kate Finch

Founder, Junior's Pantry Limited
www.juniorspantry.co.uk

Dear Entrepreneur,

ALTHOUGH SOME PEOPLE SAY YOU CAN'T LEARN to be an entrepreneur, everyone can certainly learn from other entrepreneurs, successful or not. So, to start with, congratulations on doing your homework!

A brief intro to Kabbee, the booking platform for cabs in London. Like an Expedia or Skyscanner for cabs, it gives customers a single destination for finding what they need. It launched in June 2011 after a year of development, and since then has established itself in a sector showing unusually high levels of technical change (multiple competitor launches, end to end integration) and investment (Hailo, Uber, Get Taxi, MyTaxi etc). Below are a few thoughts crystallised in this period, starting with issues within organisations followed by observations about facing the market.

A key challenge for any organisation in its infancy is allocating time and resources day to day, the flipside to developing a "big vision". Prepare to **plan and prioritise hard**: be ready to disappoint team members or potential partners/suppliers whilst being flexible enough to revisit your decisions regularly. The smaller the start-up, the more likely an external factor will be able to invalidate what was previously correct. So work on progressing areas not hostage to external events as well as those that are.

When you encounter failure, focus on wringing all the value out of it. This will help you on big decisions: do the analysis and then put it in the context of "what have we learnt?" and "does it feel right?".

As the first weeks move into months, inevitably processes need to be developed, so it is key that founders are able to package what they are doing and **hand it to others to run**. Equally, this gives newer members of the team a chance to feedback on how the business handles tasks, take ownership of their own areas and share in the goals.

Finally, on the level of team dynamics, three points. We encourage everyone to **get the tough tasks done early** in the day or week, even though it is tempting to tick off the easiest ones first. If the easy tasks don't get done, at least the big issues have taken the cream of your energy. Like in any relationship, we also find it crucial to **directly address any disputes** and ensure they are put to bed ("Let's move on"). Lastly, make sure all members of the team can **switch off occasionally**, even if only for a weekend. Headspace is a rare and precious commodity and the solution is often lurking outside the office!

In terms of facing the market, the starting point is to **listen really hard** to people's feedback and thoughts, not just in direct customer comms but also Twitter and other social media where needs and opinions are especially honest and wide ranging. Seek informal feedback from friends (even watch them engaging with the product if you can) while finding efficient ways to gather formal feedback. Immediate response to individual customers is important but identifying the bigger opportunities and shaping solutions means you are not just fire-fighting.

" Headspace is a rare and precious commodity and the solution is often lurking outside the office! "

Kabbee does not wave a mission statement in people's faces, but it is important to be able to point to what you are really trying to achieve. To reinforce this, we feel a simple and clear vision, including having business roles models ("What would x do?"), helps to provide a consistent basis for decision-making. This vision is going to change so **start with something big**, and take time to challenge and refine the detail every six months.

As a key part of much early investment is likely to be committed to customer acquisition **prepare for failure** in some marketing activities. Treat all opportunities with a healthy suspicion. Ideally test all new ideas on customers, but be realistic: sometimes you will have to have confidence in your approach and check back later to see if this was well placed. Don't only do what you can measure directly! Later, as you try to build loyalty, be ready to modify your approaches: you may get a second chance with customers but rarely a third, therefore interventions have to be quick and impactful, and you have to be seen to learn. **Nothing should be sacred**: be prepared to rewrite rules and never accept doing something one way just because it always has been done that way.

On a commercial level, **stay flexible**: study partnerships and contracts very hard, especially where you will be tied in before you see any results. Just because a company you are dealing with are big doesn't mean you have to make big commitments to them; if they won't accept your caution and wait for a bigger commitment down the line, say goodbye now.

In the end, what matters most is the entrepreneur's desire to learn and make an impact. Any early member of a team must be committed to the opportunity and spending several years deep in it. The only guaranteed reward for an entrepreneur is learning, so anyone who is not there to learn is not going to stay the course. So if you have found a challenge in an area you know you want to be submerged and make an impact in, stop to check you can commit fully to it…and then go for it.

> **❝ Never accept doing something one way just because it always has been done that way. ❞**

All the best,

Phil Makinson

On behalf of all at Kabbee

Founder and Business Development Director, Kabbee
www.kabbee.com

Kitty & Dulcie

Dear Entrepreneur,

IN 2006 I CREATED FLO & PERCY, a company designing and hand-making vintage-style hair accessories for brides. I took vintage jewellery, which I broke up and reworked into beautiful hair accessories. Every design I made for every bride was unique and no one else in the bridal market was doing the same at the time; I had cornered the market and I saw a vintage revolution coming. My designs were so much in demand I couldn't keep up with the orders. How would I make my business scalable? I decided to make the bold step of manufacturing some of the main materials I used in my designs so I could reproduce the popular designs and supply bridal boutiques. That was the turning point of Flo & Percy, and six years later we have 35 stockists and sell over 1000 headpieces a year to the higher end of the bridal market.

In 2010 I spotted another gap in the market. No one was selling online-only, budget-style fashionable wedding dresses direct to brides. I shared my idea with a close friend, Shelley Bright, and together we jointly formed Kitty & Dulcie (**www.kittyanddulcie.com**). Some of the best ideas are the most courageous and most people thought we were mad; who would buy a wedding dress online and forfeit the shopping experience? We launched in 2011 at the height of the recession and our budget-busting gowns took the bridal world by storm.

From the outset our main obstacle was to try to convey that the bride was still getting quality for a budget price. We are trying to educate the bride that shop owners have to put a significant mark-up on their dresses to cover their costs and the designers that sell to them also have to make a significant profit. By cutting out the middleman we make significant savings that we can give to our brides, hence our strapline: "Unbelievable quality, unbeatable price." We have now gained the trust of three wedding industry professionals who chose a Kitty & Dulcie for their wedding day when they could have had their pick from the industry. The testimonials we have received from them – that we will be posting on our website soon – will increase the trust significantly with our brides.

We have adopted a high-impact marketing campaign focusing on three elements: price, quality and style. No other wedding dress designer is so price focused and explicit in this regard. We advertise in the top five national wedding magazines, taking full-colour pages. We have an enviable press list via Flo & Percy who already had a strong and excellent reputation in the wedding world as a high-end brand.

Research is key to starting a business. With both companies we spent a year researching before we started. You should know your competition, if you have any, like the back of your hand. Start small and be brave. Building a fantastic website is vital and so many companies, especially the small ones, seem to overlook this.

Here were some of our main objectives:

- To offer value-for-money quality bridal dresses
- To offer fashion forward styles for the young bride
- To design and create a feminine brand with a retro look
- To design and create an eye–catching, easy to navigate website with very strong visuals including video

- To offer the same quality as 'shop bought dresses' that are 350% more expensive
- To offer a personal, friendly service with excellent customer care
- To achieve a strong relationship with the press
- To display aggressive advertising with fashionable strong images showing our price point at every opportunity
- To achieve on average a 500% mark-up
- To be able to sell internationally
- To keep things simple!

“ Start small and be brave. ”

Starting a new business is not easy, but it's fun, we have learnt so many new things and made so many new friends and above all we are making money, and that's what it is all about dear entrepreneur!

Kirstie Taylor and Shelley Carter-Bright

Founders, Kitty & Dulcie
www.kittyanddulcie.com

Dear Entrepreneur,

STARTING YOUR OWN BUSINESS CAN BE the hardest thing you ever do. It can also be the best decision you ever make.

Here are a few thoughts which have helped Little Dish become the UK's number 1 fresh, healthy food brand for toddlers and young children.

1. **Love what you do**. Many of the best businesses are those started by people who have a true passion for what they are creating. When it doesn't feel like work because you enjoy it so much.

2. **Keep it simple**. Your purpose, your vision, your values. Your objectives and your plan to get there. Your communication with your team. Don't overcomplicate things and try not to lose focus.

3. Ensure the **commercials** make sense. Make sure you have enough cash. Be willing to invest in growth.

4. **Know your customers**. Talk to your customers. Listen to your customers. People like it when you listen and give them what they ask for.

5. **Nurture and protect your brand**. Everything your business does and says should reflect what your brand stands for.

6. **Team is important**. Hire rising stars. Hire people who are smarter than you are. Work with people you trust. If someone isn't working out, make a change.

7. **Have a support system**. It could be your business partner, your husband or wife, friends or family. There will be hard days. There will be bad days. Things won't always go right. But when they do, be sure to celebrate the successes along the way.

Best of luck with your new business,

Hillary Graves

Co-founder, Little Dish
www.littledish.co.uk

Love Da Popcorn

Well hello there you funky little popper you.

FIRST, LET US INTRODUCE OURSELVES. We are Love Da Popcorn. We are three friends who met whilst working at Saatchi & Saatchi, and are now a fully (well, kind of) functioning popcorn business. We began our adventure in the summer of love that was 2010 and have been lucky enough to get our first listing in Waitrose after appearing on BBC show Dragons' Den in 2011.

Wherever we go, the question people always ask us is "why popcorn?". Well, first of all it was an accessible product. We could easily make and experiment with it in our own kitchen. Secondly, girls love popcorn – enough said on that point. Finally, and most importantly (arguably), was the opportunity for added value. Popcorn as a product and as a brand had been relatively unexplored and we felt we were just the boys to get stuck in.

Fed up of the mass-manufactured sugary crap that has dominated the market in years (we won't name names, but they sound like uttermiss!), we felt there was a gap for a fresh popcorn brand that focused on delivering a great tasting product.

But having a great product is all and well – sure if people try it and like it they might buy it again – but what is it that makes consumers buy it in the first place, and following that grow not just to buy it again, but fall in love with it. This is where branding (and the fun stuff) comes in to play. A great product combined with a compelling brand makes your product more valuable than all your competitors.

Every touch point of our brand we tailor to make sure the consumer gets a true sense of what we are about. In everything we do we aim to have infectious fun and make people smile, from our candy-striped packaging with hidden messaging under the flap, to our quirky set up at events, and even how we approach new business (we have been known to camp in receptions with balloons, banners and boxes of popcorn wrapped as Christmas presents).

This, combined with a great product at the heart of it all, gets people talking and continues to drive the business forward. However we have also picked up a few more of life's lessons along the way over the past two years…

Love Da Life's Lessons

Popcorn can come from anywhere

The idea to start making popcorn came from a competition. Christian and I were trying to win a trip to the Amazon. To do so we were using Facebook to try and find and unite 100 Bens and 100 Jerrys from around the world (guess who the competition was for), and bring them together for an event we called an urban picnic (we covered Covent Garden in 100m² of turf overnight without permission and got into a lot of trouble). Anyway, to pay for the turf we decided to make and sell….popcorn! Oh and we lost the competition.

Fail lots

In the early days, we once stayed up all night making popcorn to sell at a football game at Wembley the next day. Armed with 400 bags of popcorn over our backs, we tiredly began to sell our popcorn. After two hours we had only sold one bag, for £1. Feeling a little dejected and on our way home, we bumped into the local council who confiscated all our popcorn and the £1 from our one sale – assholes!

The answer is always "yes, of course"

There were more than a few circumstances in which we had to erm, blag a little to get new business. For our first event we pretended to be an established outfit. The cool people holding the event were from a company called Silent Cinema and they let us get onboard which meant we had less than a week to design packaging, set up a website, get a logo… and work out how to make so much popcorn. The event went well, the popcorn went down a treat, and from that we got our first paid contract.

Fail some more

Having appeared on *Dragons' Den*, we were uber excited about what lay ahead of us. Let's just say this excitement was put on hold when we realised that we hadn't trademarked our name, and in fact someone else owned it. We almost had to change our name completely until some clever lawyers got involved. Yeah, that wasn't so fun. P.S. We are now called Love Da Popcorn, not Love Da Pop.

Little boys hanging out with the big boys…

OK, so the really fun bit about being a small business is that you can be a little badass. Your bigger competitors have to be all safe and stuff so use this to your advantage. We used to go into shops and peg our labels onto competitors bags. It got us into trouble but was good fun, people loved it (especially online) and nobody sued us (we had no money – what could they sue us for?).

Try changing your name

We have all respectfully changed our names in the name of popcorn. I am pleased to introduce our legal names of Ben Jamaicanmecrazy McLaughlin, Jerry Fairlynuts Hartmann (yup, together we are Ben and Jerry – still can't believe we lost that competition) and the admirable Poppalopadingdong (the popper formerly known as Tom now has just one name, like Seal and McLovin).

Happy popping,

Martin, Christian and Tom

Founders, Love Da Popcorn
www.lovedawebsite.com

Lux Fix

Dear Entrepreneur,

WE ARE REALLY EXCITED TO BE TALKING TO YOU and telling you some of the things we have learned. We think in the order we learnt them will be useful!

At the very beginning

Get your friends to be involved – you have all those connections on places like Facebook and LinkedIn for a reason, so get them to test what you have or send them details on it so they can be among the first to be involved. It makes them feel special and gives you a readymade initial base of testers/users.

When you get started

Never take no for an answer! A real cliché but as with many completely true. Building a portfolio of luxury designers from scratch pre-launch was a big challenge – designers are approached by online

startups all the time and we had to show them why we were different and shamelessly called them again and again, until they agreed to give us a meeting.

When you need advice/connections/help

Use your network! There is not a red-blooded woman alive who will not at least read an email from someone they are introduced to who has a new and interesting business, so start having coffees and talking to friends and friends-of-friends-of-friends.

Once you have developed your first product/idea

Be passionate about it but don't necessarily believe it's The One at the cost of any perspective – if something else more exciting comes out of the work you are doing don't be afraid to capitalise on that.

The beautiful thing about starting something is you are small enough to be agile and change direction without leaving too much behind.

Love,

**Rebecca Glenapp and
Alice Hastings-Bass**

Founders, Lux Fix Ltd
www.lux-fix.com

LUX
FIX

Mama Designs

Dear Entrepreneur,

How to turn your idea for a new product into a new business

My business, Mama Designs Ltd, creates innovative baby products. So you have had a great idea for a new product but you haven't got a clue what to do next? This was the position I found myself in four years ago, when I had the idea for Mamascarf, a discreet, supportive breastfeeding cover. Here are my thoughts and the list I wish I had had:

1. **Research your market**. You might think it is a great idea but that doesn't mean anybody else will. You need to do some market research that extends further than your friends and family (who are bound to be biased and want you to succeed). As my product is baby/breastfeeding related, I asked lots of mums and mums-to-be about their experiences and thoughts about breastfeeding in public. Research can be done face-to-face in focus groups, interviews or via online surveys. Free survey sites such as SurveyMonkey are great for this. You can post a link to your survey on relevant sites and ask

people to complete it for you. It is always an idea to keep it short and concise as you will get more responses this way.

2. Once you have confirmed that your product idea is a good one you need to **get yourself a prototype**. Obviously where you get this made will really depend on the type of product. Some products will be able to be made in the UK and you will be able to take your design straight to a manufacturer/factory for them to create a prototype. If your design isn't finalised yet you may want to use a company to help you with the final design stages and creation. There are many product design consultants who can help with product design and development. You may want to get anyone who sees your product or hears your idea to sign a confidentiality agreement.

3. **Testing**. Once you have your prototype you will need to test it and carry out some further research. You may want to carry out the informal testing and further research before the formal testing is done as you may need to make some changes to your product. I would advise getting your target consumer to use your product and try it out over a period of time and get them to feedback to you. You may want to give them a series of questions to answer. Again, the type of product will determine what formal testing is required. Some products require testing by law and some are a "nice to have". Again this is something you can find out about yourself by searching online or you can get advice from a product design consultant.

4. **Protecting your design**/name with intellectual property. There are several ways of protecting your product. You can have your product name trademarked to prevent anyone else using your name. This process takes up to six months and is worth doing as soon as you decide on your product or company name. You can protect your product/design by applying for a patent or by European Design Registration. The Intellectual Property Office can provide advice and information on IP options.

5. **Finding a manufacturer**. You may want to try and find a manufacturer who is prepared to make an initial small order. This will mean that your price per item will be more expensive but hopefully you will be able to achieve economies of scale further down the line. If you choose to have your product manufactured abroad,

e.g. in China, you will need to place a large order. You can either choose to liaise direct with a factory or you may want to use an agent. These agents will have people who work in the production country and speak the language so can make the whole process much easier. However, of course this comes at a price. There are lots of companies who can help with this.

6. **Taking your product to market**. You need to decide whether you are going to launch your product yourself or use a distributor. A distributor will sell your product on your behalf to retailers. Most distributors will already sell a range of other products and you should choose a distributor who sells products that compliment yours. The benefits of using a distributor are that they will already have all of the retail contacts, trade accounts and warehousing etc. you might need in place. The downside is that you will reduce your profit margin. If you decide to sell your product yourself you will need to think about getting a website set up and how you are going to launch. Trade shows can be a great place to launch a new product as lots of retailers and buyers attend as well as relevant press contacts. I have known of some companies taking prototypes to a trade show, and then making adjustments to the final product based on buyer feedback.

7. **PR** is a great way to generate some noise about your business or product and the best thing about it is that it is free. Create a story and tailor that story for your target audience. A news desk will not be interested in the same story as a features editor but you can make your story appeal to different audiences by giving it a different slant. Stories that have worked well for me have been based around coming up with my business idea, setting up a new business after redundancy and even how my business was affected by the postal strike.

Contact some press agencies with your story – they sell stories to the national press. A press agency was interested in my story of how I came up with the idea for Mamascarf and then managed to get it in three national newspapers in one day. Follow every email up with a telephone call a day or so later. I have often found that emails or press releases have not been read until I drew someone's attention to them.

Look online for relevant media requests. Sometimes PR websites offer services where you pay a nominal amount to receive their media requests but there are sites such as Mumsnet which offer them for free. You can also use the #journorequest tag on Twitter. Think about any specific dates in the year that are relevant to your business and send out press releases or emails to journalists. Most magazines and newspapers have contact information online and you will be able to find the relevant person to contact. Remember, monthly magazines work several months ahead of newspapers.

Setting up your own business is not always easy but it can be extremely rewarding. I hope that you enjoy your journey as much as I have mine!

Keira O'Mara

Mama Designs Ltd
www.mamascarf.co.uk

MBA

Dear Entrepreneur,

THE CHINESE PHILOSOPHER LAO TZU once said, "A journey of a thousand miles begins with a single step" and with the simple act of purchasing this book the first inch of your expedition has already been conquered.

The journey you will be taking is not an uncommon one but the path will be your own and if anything this letter is just to provide some simple guidance to help you on your way.

Firstly, it is key that you know your destination. Decide where you want to end up and what you want your business to be. Is it a lifestyle business or are you trying to change the world? Be sure to align your company's mission and values to this point in everything that you do or in the end you will arrive off track.

Secondly, prepare and plan your route. Like any great expedition planning and preparation will be pivotal to its success. You must know where to point your marketing, who to target, the price to charge and where to focus your efforts. Through identifying the skills and the resources that you will need early on, you will be able to deal with the uncertainty in a more familiar and equipped manner.

Companionship on all voyages is critical and making sure that you have the right people to accompany you on yours will be fundamental. There will be people you need to help you achieve the goals for your business because they possess skills that you do not. There will be people that you need to support you personally as you push through the darkness. They are both equally important. Investors, should it be a requirement, will more readily invest in a strong team than a great individual, and having the right people to challenge your ideas as well as stand by your decisions will only increase your chances of success. Whoever these people are, remember to treat them fairly and honestly.

On your journey you will meet other travellers who you should seek to learn from and ask if they have any advice or guidance. Asking for help is not a shameful act nor does it require any lose of pride. It is simply a means of avoiding the pitfalls that others have already fallen into. Listen to their advice but remember the decisions will be yours.

Should you lose your way, then do not hesitate to turn back and try a different route. You will try lots of routes as this is the way of all great explorers. Your skill as a leader will be to determine those that work rather than those that don't.

After all the excitement, stress, disappoint and success, being able to take a step back and look at where you are and know when you have arrived is a must. This point is equally important as the first point about knowing your destination. It is only through remembering your original goal that you will be able to tell when your moment has come. Some people are great at building businesses and some are great at running large enterprises. Should this be the case then do not worry about passing the compass on as you have done all that was required of you.

66 **There will be people you need to help you achieve the goals for your business because they possess skills that you do not. There will be people that you need to support you personally as you push through the darkness. They are both equally important. 99**

Furthermore, unfortunately due to circumstances out of your control it might be possible that your destination may never be reached and that too is fine. There is no embarrassment with recognising this fact and as an American president once said, "it is the doer of deeds and not the critics that count". At no stage must you ever let one bad journey prevent you from setting out on another.

The final and most important point of view that I can share is simple. Have fun! Without the enjoyment and celebration of the achievements and milestones that you will reach, the journey will seem far longer than it really is. For the brief period we are here we must enjoy our moments in the sun and take them whenever possible. You are an explorer, a pioneer of new paths, a brave soul and this fact alone is worth celebrating.

With all this said let your journey begin and the second footstep follow the first. The fun has already started and I hope this brief note helps you to make it continue farther.

A fellow traveller,

Daniel Callaghan

Founder, MBA & Company
www.mbaandco.com

myParcelDelivery.com

❝ It is not the critic who counts: not the man who points out how the strong man stumbles or where the doer of deeds could have done better. The credit belongs to the man who is actually in the arena, whose face is marred by dust and sweat and blood, who strives valiantly, who errs and comes up short again and again, because there is no effort without error or shortcoming, but who knows the great enthusiasms, the great devotions, who spends himself for a worthy cause; who, at the best, knows, in the end, the triumph of high achievement, and who, at the worst, if he fails, at least he fails while daring greatly, so that his place shall never be with those cold and timid souls who knew neither victory nor defeat. **❞**

– Theodore Roosevelt

Dear Entrepreneur,

THIS IS GOING TO BE HARD.

You know that image you have of entrepreneurs driving fast cars, lounging on yachts with supermodels, or flying hot air balloons around the world...?

Yer, well, 99.9% of the time it isn't like that.*

99.9% of the time, you'll be up against the ropes, taking punches and just trying to stay on your feet. You'll be working longer hours than anyone else, getting paid less (if anything!) than anyone else and there will be no-one there to give you a pat on the back when you do well. You will be the only one to motivate yourself to get back in the ring each day to take another few rounds.

The one rule in entrepreneurship? Things won't go to plan.

You need to remember this and prepare for it. Be on your toes. When something doesn't go to plan and goes wrong – that's when the entrepreneur is made. That's where you need to step up to the line and be counted. If you are going to sit in the corner and cry like a baby, or chuck in the towel, then this isn't for you I'm afraid… Go work as a postman.

However, if you are going to jump straight back, face the problems and start to figure out how you are going to fix them and get back on track (or get on a different track!) – then welcome to the club my friend! You'll have earned your spurs.

So why do it? Why put yourself through all this??

The answer is simple; you'll be making meaning. You'll be building something that improves people's lives (your customers, the people that you hire, the other stakeholders in your business) and you'll be putting YOUR stamp on the world through the companies YOU help create and build. By doing this, you'll stumble across the great enthusiasms, the great devotions of which Theodore Roosevelt talks, and you will realise that you are indeed spending yourself for a worthy cause.

So go… Go spend yourself for a worthy cause. Get in the arena and open yourself up for the hits.

You'll love it, and you'll never regret doing it.

Paul Haydock

Co-Founder, myParcelDelivery.com
www.myParcelDelivery.com

*But you do have a shot at the 0.1%. Which is a lot more than the guy sitting in an office working 9-5 for a paycheck will ever have.

Naturally Cool Kids

Dear Entrepreneur,

I AM DELIGHTED AS A YOUNG UP AND COMING company to be asked about my story and how I have realised a life-long dream of running my own business.

As a child I was brought up in a self-employed family; my dad worked as many hours as it took to finish each job, my mum stayed at home to look after me and my two older brothers, but I will never forget the wonderful feeling I used to get when I was at my Dad's work with all the family helping out and working together. That has stuck with me all my life and is something I want my children to experience.

I am very big on family and putting them first which is difficult when starting a new business but I was confident I could do it. As a stay-at-home mum with a great idea I did wonder how this was going to work out, but I was at the point in my life when I was up for a challenge. I was in an ideal position to realise my dream when I won a business competition which, financially, made my idea fly and the PR surrounding it was invaluable.

In spring 2011, Naturally Cool Kids, winter and summer skincare products for children was launched. The secret? Make children's skincare fun and innovative.

We secured a large retailer within the first day of exhibiting. The response from both retailers and customers has been amazing and we now have over 50 independents, three large retailers and export to five countries, plus much, much more in the pipeline. Phew, what a difference a year makes!!

I think a lot of people with an idea are lost in the beginning, with all those thoughts like "is this really going to work?", "will people really want to buy this?", "can I give up my security to do this?". I have had many business ideas, as do lots of other people, before you settle with a great idea.

When it's right you will just know, from the feeling of excitement, that feeling in your stomach fluttering away. Then it's time to move.

Take action straightaway. Don't procrastinate as you will weaken the idea and then you may never get the business off the ground. If you feel that you hit brick wall after brick wall, don't give up. This is where I went wrong in my twenties. My husband used to ask me all the time, "Why is it that you get to a certain point with an idea then stop?". I was scared, so scared, that I would fail and embarrass myself, and then I would kick myself afterwards for being bothered about what other people thought.

❝ It is better to have tried and failed than to have failed to try… ❞
– Mike Dennison

When you are starting out, don't look too far ahead. People advise that you should write a business plan predicting the future years ahead, but for me this just didn't make sense as I feel that by taking it one step at a time and not getting too stressed out when things go wrong is the best way of dealing with things.

I have to admit that as I have dreamt of this all my life I never for one minute thought it would be as hard as it is in real life. Everyone says "aren't you lucky, working for yourself". I don't think I'm lucky. I think I've worked really hard to get to where I am with a child hanging round my neck or taking over my computer with Moshi Monsters whilst trying to speak to a buyer on the phone – a multi-tasker you have to be.

I think it is also worth remembering that having the bad days when you want to throw everything up in the air or walk away is fine. I can guarantee you there will be many such moments. But when you overcome each obstacle it does get that little bit easier and the feeling of success is well worth it. I wouldn't change it for a thing.

Enjoy your journey as there is a time for everything and this could now be yours.

Fiona Wood

Co-founder, Naturally Cool Kids
www.naturallycoolkids.com

Mum to Rhys, 17, and Finly, 6
Wife to David
xxx

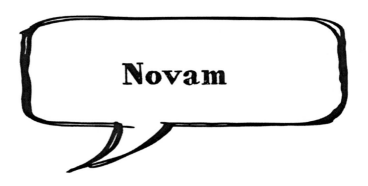

Dear Entrepreneur,

FOLLOW YOUR DREAMS AND MAKE THE MOST of everything you do. It is easy to say but few truly do for fear of failure. The truth is, being an entrepreneur will most likely be one of the hardest things you will ever do, full of emotional highs and lows, failure and success. Don't give up and continue to push forward by setting small, achievable goals and you will be surprised at how much you can achieve.

Here are some key tips for anyone starting a business:

- I often think about business ideas, but for it to be a business it needs to make money. If you think your idea is good then sanity check it by speaking to potential customers. You will soon find out if there is a market or not. Listen to them and tweak your offering if needs be. Do not just rely on family and friends for your market research as by nature they are going to be kind to you which will not do you any favours in the long run.

- Once you have done the above and you are happy take the hardest step and start the business. Believe in yourself and the business. I see too many people who do not follow through on a good idea from fear of the unknown. Start part time and generate revenue then look to go full time once the idea is proven.

■ Most people seek the full 100% of their required funding from one provider and keep getting turned down. Try this: ask for 25% from four different providers. You could even raise up to 25% from family and friends, which will only add weight to your proposal. You will be surprised how many companies will invest in you if they know someone else has.

■ If your business has not generated any revenue then you're unlikely to get a business loan. Be resourceful, look to family and friends or get a personal loan. It is risky but if you have done your homework, spoken to customers and truly believe there is a market, then why not follow your dreams.

**❝ Follow your dreams and make
the most of everything you do. ❞**

Sam Silva

Founder, Novam Ltd
www.novam.co.uk

Nuba Cocktails

Dear Entrepreneur,

IF YOU HAVE AN IDEA FOR A BUSINESS, there's just one key thing you need. One thing that will turn that idea into a business. One thing that separates those who have a business from those who don't. That thing is...

THE WILL!

Drive, motivation, perseverance. Call it whatever you want, it's vital. I hear lots of people say they've got an idea but they endlessly procrastinate for whatever reason. These people are doomed to failure. You've already taken the first step and bought this book – but don't let that be the last.

A driven person will do everything in their power to make their business work.

Having a business is brilliant, and can be hugely rewarding. For me, as a self-confessed control freak, I knew it was the only way forward! It's the little things, like being in control of what I wear, where I work, when I work, that bring me a surprising amount of joy! But don't kid yourself... instead of being a slave to a boss, I've become a slave to my business.

Being successful is completely different to having the drive to turn an idea into a business. There are plenty of other skills that you will need to succeed. But if you're driven and committed, you will learn what they are and train yourself accordingly!

And it's hard. Much harder than you think it will be. Being driven to succeed is what keeps me going.

❝ You've already taken the first step and bought this book but don't let that be the last. ❞

There are so many sacrifices you need to make to start your business, and to keep it going. I don't mean to sound all doom and gloom – starting my business was the best thing I've ever done – but tough times always lie ahead and you need to be prepared for that. People tell you that having a business is hard but it's impossible to comprehend just what that means until you're doing it yourself.

Be prepared to sacrifice everything. When everything is gone, your drive is all you have left and you need to rely on that to see you through.

The ironic thing is that I think I'm inherently lazy – I wanted to start my business because I don't want to work! At least not beyond the age of 35 anyway. Drive can help you to overcome your weaknesses! But drive can be mentally and physically tiring.

Therefore have a long think about what you really want. If you want it, I mean really, really want it, then you will go for it, and not because anyone tells you to. Only you and your drive can make you succeed.

Best of luck guys!

Vicky Novis

Founder and Managing Director,
Nuba Cocktails
www.nubacocktails.com

OGL Marketing

Dear Entrepreneur,

IT'S A REAL HONOUR TO SHARE WHAT I HAVE LEARNT and give advice to fellow entrepreneurs.

I am 20 years old, I am running my first business, which is 9 months old and going really well, and I have learnt a huge amount about myself, other people and business.

The biggest piece of advice I could give is don't be scared to learn from your mistakes. I went into my business blind. It was an industry I didn't know too much about and for my first job I heavily relied on other people's experience – luckily it went to plan. On other occasions I have made huge mistakes, cold-calls that now make me cringe, bad judgement, trying to maximise profits and letting quality slip.

> **❝ It's hard work but one day it will all be worth it. ❞**

I have made every mistake in the book, but I will never make the same mistake twice and now I am doing great! Lots of happy customers and a great reputation.

For me personally, it's been a bumpy journey. I remember being at a networking event knowing that if I accidentally swore, I couldn't afford to pay the £1 fine. It's hard and stressful, but now and then I feel on top of the world and all the stress has been worth it.

Set yourself goals, work hard and enjoy the journey!

It's hard work but one day it will all be worth it.

Oliver Luke

Founder, OGL Marketing
www.oglmarketing.co.uk

OGL
Marketing

What's the problem?

WHEN THINKING ABOUT STARTING YOUR BUSINESS it is crucial to really pinpoint the problem you are trying to solve. You need to be able to describe what you are doing in no more than a sentence that will catch people's attention.

■ Come up with a simple, one sentence description of your new business which explains the problem it solves.

Be different

What is going to get customers to choose you over a competitor? Think about how you can make yourself stand out. Don't compete on price. As a startup you can provide a superior customer service experience to larger competitors – concentrate on service rather than price cuts.

■ Compete with superior customer service rather than on lower prices.

Agile

There has never been a better time to start a software company; you can leverage open source products and scale them cheaply in the cloud. You no longer need to invest in expensive software licenses and server hardware. Use technologies like Ruby On Rails , Twitter, Bootstrap to rapidly prototype your idea and deploy it to a cloud environment such as Heroku or Amazon EC2.

- Build on open source technologies and use cheap cloud infrastructure.

Get it out there

Online software moves fast, you need to work on getting a minimum viable product (MVP) online and in front of potential customers as soon as possible. Building your product in stealth mode for months or even years will not only mean it is outdated when released but also that it may not match your customers' needs. By getting a rough initial version in front of customers as soon as possible you can quickly build in new features and respond to customer demands.

- Get a version of your product out there quickly and update it based on customer feedback.

Get big name customers

Getting some recognisable brands using your product early can have a huge impact on convincing other customers to trust you with their business. Use LinkedIn and Rapportive to locate the right people inside an organisation and contact them offering them a free trial period or heavily discounted promotional price. Get testimonials and quotes for use on your website.

- Get big name brands to use your system by offering free trials and discounts – they will hope grow your customer base.

Branding

Giving your new project a professional look through a well-designed brand identity is crucial. To start off with it may well just be you in your bedroom, but with the right brand you can project the image of being an already established market player your customers can trust. Services like 101 Designs can help you get a top class brand identity without having to spend a fortune. Test out designs on friends and potential customers and update based on their feedback.

■ Hire a designer to build a quality brand to project the image that you are bigger than you really are. Test it on friends.

Revenue

It is crucial to ensure your startup is built to start producing revenue straightaway. Don't expect the banks or Silicon Valley style VCs to help you at this stage. Having a profitable product will not only help you grow the business without having to rely on anyone else, it also puts you in a much better negotiating position should you want to seek debt financing or venture capital in the future.

■ Don't rely on VCs or banks for finance – build your product to be revenue-generating from the start.

James Wood

Founder, PageHub
www.pagehub.co.uk

The Pilates Pod

THE PILATES POD IS A SPECIALIST PILATES STUDIO offering small Pilates Matwork Classes and 1:1 personal training in Hitchin, Hertfordshire. We started the business in July 2011, renting some space in a local osteopathic clinic and within six months had moved into our own premises. We have just expanded our timetable to be able to offer sessions seven days a week.

The decision to start our own business came about a few months after our first son was born. I had returned to work from maternity leave, and working a 9 to 5 job no longer offered the flexibility we needed as a family.

Starting-up

At the time it seemed like a big, risky decision to go it alone, especially with a young family. But we did our research, looked at the market, researched competitors and committed ourselves to going through with it. My husband is a graphic and web designer, so with our combined skills we were able to do nearly everything ourselves. This meant that we were able to keep costs very low. By using social media and engaging with the local business community, we were able to quickly establish our brand and raise interest and awareness of our services, and within a few hours of going live we were already selling classes. From then on, we felt confident that we had made the right decision.

I would say our three biggest selling points were our expertise, our brand and our location.

Expanding

Knowing how, and when to expand the business is quite tricky. We didn't want to stretch ourselves too far too soon. We asked our clients what they wanted and when, and acted on their feedback. It's really important to be decisive when you're setting up a business, and to follow through with your ideas. We have always been very cautious about our projections; so as long as your most pessimistic forecast holds up financially, then it's time to go for it.

Branding

When we were operating one a half days a week we had the expertise in Pilates, even if we didn't have large impressive premises at the time. We used our branding to great effect to reassure our clients that even though we were small, we were excellent at what we were doing. Having a distinct, recognisable brand also helps to build awareness. Sometimes it can take many months to convert someone into a paying customer, so exposing people subconsciously to your business as often as possible is very important.

People

As a service-based business, the importance having great people onboard is incalculable. With a small team, everything everyone does affects the business, so it's vitally important to make sure your team is happy, well-trained and engaged. Get a good bookkeeper and accountant onboard as early as possible. But it's not just the employees who affect the business.

By building great relationships with other local businesses, council members, clients and the public, you can achieve much more than you can on your own. This can also provide amazing PR and media opportunities.

Online

I struggle to think how we could have started a business before the internet and social networks were available. Use them strategically and plan your campaigns. Our approach is that everything we do online, whether it's on Facebook, Twitter or on your own website, reflects our passion, excitement and enthusiasm for our business. And best of all, it's practically free to do.

Do it!

Starting our own business has been an incredible, exciting journey. It's been very hard work, especially at the beginning. We work 15 to 16 hours a day most days of the week, but when it's your own business it somehow doesn't feel the same. Being able to make your own decisions, being inventive and creative are massive rewards, and if all goes to plan you should feel the benefit financially too. One day!

Michelle Smith

Director, The Pilates Pod Ltd
www.thepilatespod.co.uk

Pimlico Plumbers

Dear Entrepreneur,

PEOPLE HAVE BEEN TELLING ME FOR AGES that my story is interesting and that maybe I should write a book about how I managed to end up a millionaire despite growing up on one of south London's roughest estates, and bunking off school whenever I got the chance.

To me it doesn't seem that interesting; basically I wanted to be a plumber since I was seven years old. The only bloke round our way back when I was a kid who had any money, a decent car (a Ford Zephyr), and could afford to go on holiday, was Bill, the local plumber. He used to give me two bob a day to help him, so I started bunking off school. To me, like most of the things I've done over the years, it was a no-brainer – miss school, make some cash! I guess it's a good thing Bill wasn't a bank robber or I might have ended up in an all together different style of Big House.

After I officially left school, when I was 15, again it was no real decision for me . . . I always wanted to be a plumber, so I got an apprenticeship, and that was that. It was soon pretty obvious to me that leaving school at 15 was the worst decision of my life – I really should have done it a year earlier. I guess that was one of the first lessons I learned in life and business – once you believe you know the right answer, don't waste time, get on with it! People are always trying to arrange 'meetings' with me about things, in fact they seem more focussed on getting into my office than in telling me why. Most of the time I can save them the bus fare, if they'd only come out and tell me what it was they wanted. Call it a strength or a weakness, but I've always been someone who makes decisions quickly, one way or another.

I never really set out to become a millionaire, or even had much of an idea other than to earn a good living and provide some of the things I never had growing up for my family. From day one as a self-employed plumber and heating engineer, as I drove my old van to work, that was the plan. And the way I believed I could achieve that was to be the best plumber, offering the best service possible. It didn't seem like a complicated plan; all I did was get up every day and go to work, work hard, charge a fair price and give people more reasons to get me back (or tell their friends to) than not to. That's still the way I run Pimlico Plumbers today.

Things have obviously changed quite a bit since the '70s; the vans have got a whole lot better for a start. Also the company turns over £17 million and employs more than 200 people. My role no longer involves being on the tools, although I sometimes think the hours only get worse as you get more successful. What hasn't really changed is the fact that my family's livelihood (and those of all those who work for me) continue to rely on people phoning us when they need some plumbing done. We also now employ electricians, carpenters, builders, roofers, drain technicians and experts in the repair of small appliances.

For my part, running Pimlico Plumbers is a huge task, and while I don't unblock many (actually any) toilets, I do spend a good deal of my time maintaining the reputation of the company, and making sure potential customers know who we are, and that we're the best. The first part means that we can't just have any old person working for us, they need to fit. They need to look good in the uniform, clean shaven, no tattoos, we also CRB all new employees. But more than that they need to not only be top class tradesmen, but they also need to be ambassadors for the company, be problem solvers, cool heads in a crisis, in short someone who our customers can trust to look after their homes. And believe me, finding such people is as difficult as it is crucial to our survival.

The other thing I get involved with is the promotion of the company through radio, television, newspapers and social media. People ask me why I, a plumber by trade, bother with all this kind media work. The answer is that nothing has really changed since the early days when I relied on doing a good job, and word of mouth hopefully did the rest. We still do an exemplary job of course, and customer recommendations are still hugely important to us, but with the power of the press we can get the message of what we are about through to far more people.

Charlie Mullins

Founder, Pimlico Plumbers
www.pimlicoplumbers.com

Pleasecycle

RY MORGAN IS CO-FOUNDER AND CEO of PleaseCycle, a start-up which combines cycling, digital technology and "gamification" to help organisations get more staff commuting by bike. Ry graduated from the University of St. Andrews in 2010 with a first in Management, but whilst there he was heavily involved with the Scottish Institute for Enterprise, completed a three-month Enternship in London, and dabbled in a variety of pet projects. The following anecdotes stem from his journey of "Entern to Entrepreneur":

❝Only in growth, reform, and change, paradoxically enough, is true security to be found. ❞
– Anne Morrow Lindbergh (1906-2001)

This for me epitomises the mindset of entrepreneurs. At the very least it's certainly what lured me into the world of start-ups; an ever malleable future that never cements, never stagnates, and never stops surprising. I dreaded the quintessential "corporate career path" after graduating: set-salaries, set-promotions, set-schedule, set-appraisals, set-five-years-of-my-life – yikes. The thought that the next six-months are in my hands – for better or for worse – is an irreducibly invigorating thought. A lot of people would say entrepreneurship is perhaps the least secure job prospect out there – I guess it depends on how much you back yourself. Constantly learning, forever evolving, an ever-shifting roller-coaster ride of professional endeavours – I find the utmost of security in that insecurity.

66 You'll learn more in those two days than you would in two years at business school. 99

The above quote is from the Steve Jobs' biography, and sees Jobs asking his son to attend 48 hours of meetings at Apple, notably valuing the hands-on experience greater than 24 months at college. I couldn't agree more. I spent the summer of 2009 enterning (**www.enternships.com**) at CURB Media and learnt more about business, start-ups and advertising in those few months than during my whole degree. Thrown in at the deep-end, by the second week I was handling accounts for clients such as Waitrose, attending meets with agencies like TBWA\, and given enough autonomy to create an entirely new type of media – bioluminescent bacteria – which went on to be used in campaigns by Johnson & Johnson and Warner Bros. I speak from experience when saying that you will learn far more by "getting out there" and "doing it" than any number of months spent planning, strategising, reading, building or talking about your idea.

66 Luck is a mindset. 99

You often hear stories of entrepreneurs who "created their own luck" or were simply "in the right place at the right time" – I personally think it has a lot to do with the mindset of certain individuals. Richard Wiseman conducted a study on "luck" in 2011 in which he asked two groups of people to read a newspaper and count how many pictures were inside.

Group A considered themselves "unlucky," whilst conversely Group B felt "lucky." It took Group A an average of two minutes to count the pictures, whereas it took Group B mere seconds. Why? Because on the second page of the newspaper was the message: "Stop counting. There are 43 photographs in this newspaper." The point I'm trying to make is that "lucky" people see what is there, rather than just what they are looking for. If you remain open to opportunity, networking, new ideas and fresh thinking – which I'd argue most entrepreneurs are – then you can indeed weight the dice in your favour.

❝ If you're 100% happy with the product when it launches, you've waited too long. ❞

Eric Rees, author of *The Lean Startup*, lauds the benefits of launching Minimum Viable Products, i.e. the most basic form of your value proposition, and then iterating/adapting quickly based on customer feedback. This allows you to (a) get going, the benefits of which I've already specified above; (b) test your business hypothesis before you've spent a lot of physical/financial resource on the venture; (c) gather valuable advice and criticism to aid further development before it's too late; and (d) pivot to a slightly different value proposition should (a), (b) or (c) alter your initial assumptions about the marketplace. PleaseCycle originally launched as a physical service provider (e.g. training, maintenance, parking) yet we rapidly realised that in order to deliver this we'd need a digital "hub" to engage with clients. This led to the creation of our Cycle Hub® system which has ultimately become our main product and seen us pivot into essentially a software company. No amount of market research, strategising or planning can unearth such tacit insights.

Ry Morgan

Founder, PleaseCycle

www.pleasecycle.com

Poikos

Dear Entrepreneur,

Open palms or folded fists

EVERY INDIVIDUAL PERSON'S LIFE is a story of influence, connection, and consequences. Every unique life discerns its own truths, its own purpose(s). It is a deeply personal struggle with the fundamental energies of the universe.

Some choose to harness those energies for destruction, triumph, laying waste to life and nature for cruel aggrandisement. Others channel their fire into forging alliances and networks, into laying foundations for incredible pursuits, which, on occasion, they may never themselves live long enough to fully enjoy.

Some time ago, I was exploring the newfound freedoms in being an adult. I thought about my life, and the things and people that I love, and hold dear to me. I considered that if I have but one life to lead, it was a precious and finite resource, to be spent on somehow improving the world, on leaving it in a better shape in which I had found it.

I thought of becoming a surgeon, and healing perhaps 10,000 in a long career. That would be a noble way to spend a life, surely. However, upon deep reflection I decided that I must become an entrepreneur; because entrepreneurship is perhaps the only sure way to change the world for the better.

Really? Yes, only you know how your own shoes pinch. By being an entrepreneur, you provide opportunities for others to make choices about how they wish to spend their money. That money goes to your suppliers, and sends invisible waves of information around the world. These waves of information are the emergent property of billions of individuals making their own independent, individual decisions on how to improve their personal human existence.

Through entrepreneurship, positive and beneficial joys of the world are magnified. One entrepreneur can have an immeasurable impact upon the lives of everyone on this planet.

Human progress, and the minimisation and mitigation of suffering, cannot come from anything but free and mutually beneficial trade. Tragically however, our civilisation is built around the concept of some people producing wealth, and other people plundering it.

There are fundamentally two classes within society: Those who create, and those who farm.

Most of society's wealth is concentrated in the hands of those who farm – be it land, favours and privileges, or capital. Through accident of birth, through deceit, or election and the use of force, they tightly grip the commanding heights of society and lease the benefits thereof to the highest bidder.

This is the way of the human farm, to which practically everyone on the planet is in bondage.

This is the way where men are free-range livestock, where unlike an animal, they respond to the mere whisper of a threat.

This is the way of cruelty and cages, constant violence and ceaseless monopolies on mass murder.

This is the way of thieves and slavers.

This is the way of state and politics.

There is another class, one where producers acquire wealth legitimately and fairly, through hard work, pragmatism, and providing things of value.

This is the way of peaceful co-operation and mutually beneficial arrangements.

This is the way where production of valuable new benefits for the world causes people to willingly pay for them.

This is the way which creates a better tomorrow for our children, and ignites healthy change.

This is the way of true heroes and champions.

This is the way of the entrepreneur.

Tell me, friend, which way will you choose to live?

Nell Watson

Futurist, voluntaryist, technologist and disruptive innovator. One who is deeply nostalgic for a peaceful era, which has yet to come.

www.poikos.com

Poke London

THERE IS NO FORMULA TO BEING AN ENTREPRENEUR. What I can share with you, though, is what works for me.

I didn't start with a lust to create businesses, hunting for niches to exploit. I started with an idea that I couldn't not do.

Hulger was born from an idea I had in 2002, which was plugging an old phone handset into a mobile phone. I hacked a quick prototype together and took it out on the streets to see how people reacted. They went MENTAL! So I knew I was onto something and I took great pleasure in eliciting this reaction. I set up a site to share the idea, really cheaply and simply. It fanned the flames and a couple of years later I was on a double page spread in the *New York Times*.

I had reached a crossroads: Either take the idea to a production model and build a brand around it, or leave it for someone else to do and then deal with the horror every time I saw someone else profiting from my idea. Somewhat reluctantly I took the former road. I knew it was going to be a mass of hard work but the alternative wasn't stomachable. The noisy phone idea helped us build the brand and distribution channels so when the Plumen light bulb idea came along, we could scale pretty fast. It quickly took over as a much more potent product and continues to grow steadily nearly two years after launch.

I'm now seven years into establishing the Hulger company and there are a few things to reflect on which could be useful.

The first and most important is we (Michael-George my business partner and I, and later Ronnie Renton, our chairman) never did this for the money. We were driven by the will to see our idea out there in the world, being enjoyed and changing things for the better. We wanted to make people smile, but we also wanted to use our products as a tool to drive a consumption that was positive for the planet, not the other way round as is so often the case with things that only add to the landfill. Money would be the enabler, the fuel to allow things to scale and new ideas to be born. Staying close to this cause has also kept up our motivations, day in and day out. When you hit a massive bump in the road it's easier to get over knowing you're still crystal clear about what we're doing and what's really driving your passion. Greed can keep you going for a while but it's nowhere near as motivating and sustainable as a deep-rooted interest in what you're trying to achieve.

Nicolas Roope

Founder, Poke London
www.pokelondon.com
www.plumen.com

Safer Minicabs

Dear Entrepreneur,

IN JANUARY 2008 I WAS THINKING OF IDEAS for my final year dissertation at Kingston University whilst I studied my BSc (Hons) Software Engineering degree. I came up with the simple idea of an app for booking a minicab and getting the best fares in a single place. I was awarded a 1st class for this project.

Before I started I needed to understand how to take an idea to market. I learnt various things on my journey to make this materialise, which I want to share with fellow entrepreneurs.

Most importantly, before you start your journey you need to be very clear on what you aim to develop. This means knowing what your product will look like (doesn't need to be final but have a vision), how it will work, who needs to be involved, identifying costs and skills required, and so on.

Next it's about how you will actually make it happen. To build a product, take it to market and ensure you are satisfying customers you will need outside support but also critical advice to take you through the journey. What I mean is go and get a mentor who will help you on your journey and will not only say all the good things but also all the things that can go wrong with your idea and your strategies. You need a mentor who will challenge you and not only wants to help but also has an interest in ensuring you succeed, and they do that by asking you tough questions and challenging you. Remember, if you don't agree with your mentor then always counter-challenge them; it's beneficial for you both to get a good understanding and take the good advice on board and leave aside the advice you don't think is relevant. As a quick example of this, I started with my first mentor who challenged my idea in many ways and helped me think about business plans, models, revenue options, partnerships and much more. What this did was gave me the foundation to map out my product and vision very clearly. I then went on to find more mentors and build more contacts. This is absolute key when starting out – get in front of as many people as you can, go and network, ask for help and don't be afraid. If you feel that asking someone for their help or free advice is being cheeky then let it be, but until you ask you never know. I cannot stress enough how important networking, building strong relationships and having mentors is. Safer Minicabs has been mentored by Executive Directors of Virgin Media in Operations, Brand, Marketing, Commercial and Sales along with mentors from Ernst & Young, Shell and Logica, who all bring different expertise to the table in directing the company.

I was at an awards ceremony and seeing two potential mentors who were judges I went over and introduced myself and told them about my idea. They sent a few challenges my way and we got on, so I asked the question, "Would you mind giving me your views as I develop this idea?". The answer was yes. They continued supporting me and the following year I won one of the awards. As part of this I maintained a good working relationship. Managing a pool of contacts and relationships with business contacts and mentors is very important.

Don't be afraid of negative comments from mentors and business professionals; some will intentionally do it to put you off on starting out because they hadn't spotted the opportunity. When I started Safer Minicabs I went to three individuals; one from Addison Lee, a board director for Transport for London and an experienced innovations director at Business Link. They all thought I was mad and told me that the product was not needed in an industry which is run by "giants" with "millions of pounds" at their disposal. I was also told that apps are not the way forward!

> **❝ I cannot stress enough how important networking, building strong relationships and having mentors is. ❞**

I learnt one thing, and that is every time someone says something, take it on board, evaluate why they said it and think about what you're trying to do and see how it adds up. If what you think does not match up, then you have your answer, which means you should ignore their advice and carry on. If you find that they are right then find a solution to tackle the issue or move on and try something else. But always do evaluate input and never be put off by someone saying you shouldn't do it. I went back to these guys afterwards and they were shocked one – even asked me to speak at an event!

My last piece of advice is to listen carefully to your customers and research on what they want. You have to take into consideration that if an idea only works in the way you envision it and you won't compromise then there is no point in selling your product or service to businesses or consumers. They are paying so take their feedback, adapt and improve. A very important part of this is to set ground rules, i.e. how far you will take their feedback and when you will action it. Suggestions will come through all the time but as an entrepreneur and company leader you have to decide on the order in which you will tackle things.

Finally, be focused with your vision and ideas. Every day you will wake up and have new ideas but my mentors taught me to focus. If you focus you will achieve better results than trying an idea for two weeks and then trying something else the following week. Always stay focused and see the tasks fully through to completion.

Best of luck, enjoy the journey and I hope your hard work and efforts pay off.

Jayesh Hirani

CEO, Safer Minicabs

www.safeminicab.com

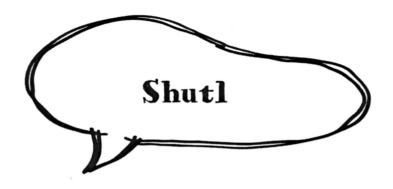

MY ADVICE TO ANY ASPIRING ENTREPRENEUR considering making the plunge is… Don't do it!

At least not yet.

As far as life decisions go, there aren't many that are bigger or that have more far-reaching consequences than starting-up. If you are successful, many people's livelihoods will be in your hands and if you're not, your commitment will feel like it was for nothing… or worse.

It's not easy either, ⅔ new businesses fail within their first three years. Beating these odds requires a 24/7 commitment. Until you are ready, willing and able to give it, you should not consider setting off down that path. And to be clear, this is not a commitment you should give lightly.

Success is more about what you don't do than what you do do, making due diligence paramount. The secret to good due diligence is that it only works before you have made any real commitment, which will otherwise obscure your objectivity. Entrepreneurs are blind to clouds, but never silver linings.

The trick is to do due diligence before you are an entrepreneur. For me this means doing everything possible to determine whether a prospective venture will fail before you and others commit your lives to it.

Step 1 is to ensure that your product/service is solving a big enough problem so that your prospective customers will buy it. This does not

> **Failure is never to be feared, indeed it should be welcomed because the faster you can fail, the more time you have left for success.**

mean telling your friends, family and acquaintances about your fantastic idea (although of course you should), rather it means finding and then selling your solution to real customers – people you've never met whose money you will need if you are to be successful. Only once you are convinced they will buy at a price high enough for you to make a profit you are ready to move on.

Step 2 is to determine how big the market for your product/service is – quantify how many potential customers there are and whether the opportunity is growing (or shrinking). And whether there are competitors already in the market and if there are, how are they doing? Competitors are not to be feared – in fact they should be welcomed as validators of demand (worrying if you are entering what you think is a big market that has no competitors). The market is, in most cases, the most important factor in the success of your venture and it is a tide you cannot beat.

Step 3 is to figure out what you would need in order to be able to take the product/service to market. If you will need skills and experience that you don't have, then now is the time to seek them out. A good idea without a team to execute it is useless.

Once you have completed steps 1-3 and still feel confident – that's when you are ready to take the plunge. To beat the odds, you need to give yourself the highest probability of success before you start. It is hard enough without a headwind but a tailwind can make all the difference. Failure is never to be feared, indeed it should be welcomed because the faster you can fail, the more time you have left for success.

Tom Allason

Founder, Shutl
www.shutl.com

Silence Breakers

Dear Entrepreneur,

FIRST OF ALL, I'M SURE WE CAN ALL ADMIT that we're not just speaking from personal experience. We're speaking from others' experiences as well. I've learned so much from other entrepreneurs, and most of it just reinforces what I can say here. It's good to check back and take note of what others have said. One successful entrepreneur once said, "If you have a Plan B, you shouldn't be working on Plan A." I tend to agree. Live, breathe, sleep, eat, drink your entrepreneurial plan. Be excited about it. If you don't, don't do it. As my mother always says, "If in doubt – don't."

The most important thing, above all else, is having passion for what it is you're doing – absolute unshakable passion. Believe in it and let your heart guide you, before kicking your head into gear (the head's pretty useful, so let's not understate that). Gut instinct is not to be trivialised either. Every single time I've thought that my gut was being unfair, and that I ought to give something else a chance, I've come back to the realisation that I should have given more trust to that gut instinct. If you get a bad feeling in your belly about something, avoid.

Keep control. It might surprise some that I'm not going to advocate all the creative commons stuff or trivialise intellectual property, but this is very important: you are the entrepreneur, which means that your enterprise is your baby. It's all well and good others calling themselves team players and being there for you, but it's your behind when it goes wrong. So be the boss. Be proud. And keep control. It's yours. Own it.

Surround yourself with **people you trust completely.** However, don't just pick people because you like them or they do other good things in your life. They have to be the right people on the bus that you're driving. You also have to choose your collaborators wisely; don't just work with people because you'd like to help them as there might not be a great deal in return for you. I've spent too much of my time being loyal, giving people more chances, and listening to lip service. Be good, be ethical, but do not ever compromise your own vision and strategy for others.

Strategy, hmm. **Be patient, and plan.** This means having a long-term strategy, and breaking it down into short-term chunks so you have a realistic route to where you want to be. All the little successes add up in the long run. Remember to celebrate your achievements, too. It's bloody difficult being an entrepreneur, and when you're in the heat of it, it's easy to forget how hard you've actually worked at times.

Don't be too cautious. Be prepared to take chances. Fear of failure separates the brave from the cowards, and all cowards have ever done is existed to get by. It's good to take calculated risks. Challenge yourself, give yourself goosebumps. Do something that scares you. Do not be afraid of failure; it's pointless.

❝ The most important thing, above all else, is having passion for what it is you're doing absolute unshakable passion. ❞ It's perhaps worth noting that most successful entrepreneurs have had at least one significant failure in their past. I believe it was Woody Allen who said, "If you're not failing every now and again, it's a sign you're not doing something very innovative." He also said, "I don't want to achieve immortality through my work; I want to achieve it through not dying." So this is a guy who makes sense. Take notice. Dust yourself off, pick yourself up, and battle on.

Be clear, be honest, and absolutely make sure the expectations of those you're working with are realistic. And for the love of all things holy, get a contract: no matter who they are, how reliable they may be, how trustworthy they seem, how well you know them, or even whether they babysit your kids or you saved their life: **contracts...always**.

Oh, and in the business world, it's important to admit when you don't understand a TLA (three letter acronym). Most people make up that crap to make themselves sound better.

Jay Baker

Managing Director, SilenceBreakers
www.silencebreakers.org

Gavin Smith

So, what's your excuse? Lack of time, money, ideas maybe? Whatever the excuse, most reasons come down to fear. Fear of making a fool of ourselves, of losing money or wasting time. Fear stops many of us from taking the hardest step which is of course the first, but action cures fear.

Let's have a look at some of these excuses. **Lack of time?** You had time to read this far and that could have been put towards starting your business. We also tend to waste lots of time browsing the internet or watching television. Make time.

Lack of money? A restaurant can cost hundreds of thousands to start, but have you stripped the idea to its core? Start small, what about starting a catering truck? You can prove the concept more cost-effectively and in various locations and the overheads are almost non-existent when compared to a 'proper' restaurant. It will also be easier to get funding should you decide to become a 'proper' restaurant. If you do happen to fail you will also have less to lose and can start again.

Lack of ideas? Don't reinvent the wheel. It works fine. 99% of ideas are two existing ideas put together to create something new: Ebay – an auction but online, Netflix – video rentals to you, Subway – McDonalds for sandwiches, the wind up radio. etc. None of these businesses invented something new. Auctions, video rentals, sandwiches and radios all existed long before those businesses got going.

Once you have an idea, don't keep it a secret. Ask people what they think and don't be paranoid about people stealing it – they won't. You can't protect ideas but they're not really worth protecting. Record companies existed before Richard Branson started Virgin – if he had spoken to you about starting it, you would unlikely create one just as successful – the idea is just part of the whole package. You stand to have a lot more ideas if you share and develop them rather than keep it a secret.

I'm also going to briefly mention passion. Everybody seems to be talking about passion and its importance in business. If your neighbour is making a lot of money in their own business then don't think you can copy them and be just as successful. Why? Because they love what they do and if all you want to do is make a fortune from it, then you'll fail. They love whatever it is they do. They eat, sleep and breathe it.

James Dyson, creator of the bagless vacuum cleaner, famously created 5127 prototypes. He was fanatical about creating the best vacuum cleaner in the world. He wouldn't have created thousands of prototypes if he wasn't passionate about the concept.

Finally, sales. Without sales you don't have a business. Some think that selling is manipulative, annoying and/or boring but it is actually helping, sociable and about learning. If you think that selling is something you would never be able to do then just remember that you sell yourself your whole life – not just in business. You sell yourself to a potential employer, to a customer, to a girlfriend/boyfriend – you're not manipulating them you are just showing yourself in the best possible light. If asked your greatest weakness at a job interview it's unlikely you'll say, "I'm extremely lazy, always late and easily distracted". You're far more likely to say the vomit-inducing "I'm a perfectionist" or "I'm a workaholic" as it looks and sounds better. You know yourself better than anyone, you're the only one who can truly sell you. It's the same in business. If you can't afford to employ others then you need to sell and it's probably best, as you know the product better than anyone. If you hate selling, it's absolutely in your interest to

> **" If all you want to do is make a fortune from it, then you'll fail. "**

> **The only thing stopping you from starting is you.**

get over it. It'll be more useful than just getting extra sales and, like any skill, the more you do it the better you get at it.

Remember that the only thing stopping you from starting is you. There's an endless list of excuses not to do something but my view is it's better to try and fail than to be always thinking 'what if?' As Sir Richard Branson puts it:

> **The brave may not live forever but the cautious do not live at all.**

Regards,

Gavin Smith

Entrepreneur

Dear Entrepreneur,

Why did you start your business?

SnoozeShade came about because, like all mums, I needed to get out after having my daughter, who in turn needed her sleep! When I was pregnant I was in a wheelchair for the final three months and for three months after my daughter's birth.

Once I could walk again I just wanted to get out as much as I could. When she was tiny, popping out was easy as she slept deeply and often. As she got older, it became harder for her to switch-off – or she would be easily woken by light or noise.

I needed a solution. So I searched the internet for a suitable product... and I couldn't find a thing. Many products let in too much light, sunshades were too bulky and baby could still see out.

One day, I rather foolishly said to a few friends that someone should invent something – so they said 'go on then'.

I developed SnoozeShade, a universally-sized, breathable blackout blind for prams and pushchairs with UPF50+ sun protection.

Following a successful trade show, I took SnoozeShade from being a working prototype to being on sale in the UK and endorsed by several highly-regarded UK baby magazines in just four months. Now a multinational brand, it sells in most major UK retailers and in more than 20 countries worldwide. The range has grown to include seven products and we have more in development.

What motivated you through the hard times?

Bringing the SnoozeShade range to market has been stressful, bringing me perilously close to complete exhaustion on a couple of occasions, but I believe my determination saw me through these difficult periods.

I'm an ideas person and am passionate about my business, my products and making life easier for parents/carers. I know, as a mum myself, that being able to get out and about with small children is vital, particularly in the early years.

Is there anything you would do differently if you were to start another business?

I would use more childcare, to free up more time to work on growing my business, rather than juggling a few hours of nursery here and there. Trying to work flat out getting the work done of ten people yourself is made so much harder with a little toddler 'working' with you. I believe childcare is just as important as advertising and should be a legitimate business expense that I would recommend any budding entrepreneur to invest in.

Also, when your business starts to flourish, try to find a balance between work and rest. There just aren't enough hours in the day. I work full time, with help from a few very part-time consultants, but with things growing so fast, it is often difficult to switch off at night. It has taken time to realise that if I don't give myself time off, I won't be able to give SnoozeShade the energy it needs.

Do you have any money-saving tips?

I'm always a fan of saving money and must admit to being a social media junkie – free publicity is very welcome and the power of word-of-mouth should never be underestimated. I use Facebook and Twitter constantly to share advice, tips, pictures, product info and relevant or amusing stories and love the personal connection it gives me with SnoozeShade fans.

Do you have some final top tips?

Research – if you have an idea, research it with your family and friends and search and search on the internet. Just because something already exists or has existed and failed in the past, don't let it put you off. Times and markets change and you may well be able to deliver on elements where others have failed such as marketing knowledge, financial investment, the right manufacturer or even just time. Innovation is key, so keep researching as your product develops and evolves and don't be afraid of change.

The most important thing to do with any business is to establish your USP – Unique Selling Point – and make sure you truly understand why you're different or better.

Good luck and have fun!

Cara Sayer

Managing Director, SnoozeShade
www.snoozeshade.com

Socialable

Dear Entrepreneur,

THERE IS SO MUCH I COULD SAY TO YOU, but I appreciate how overwhelming it can be if you have too much advice when you start a new venture. Therefore I'm going to focus my advice on three things:

1. How to stay motivated
2. Trusting your gut
3. How to use networking

First, let me congratulate you on taking this brave step. Whatever your age it is not easy to go against the grain and decide that you are going to be in charge of your own destiny. We are conditioned to believe that the only sensible way to get ahead is to get a good education and then secure a great job. So people will look at you like you've gone nuts. Especially given the bleak economic forecast we keep hearing about these days.

Therefore my first piece of advice to you is to hold onto the passion, the drive or whatever motivated you to take this step and keep hold of it tight.

Whilst I don't want to put you off just as you are beginning, I do need to be honest with you. The path you have chosen is best described as a roller-coaster packed full of corkscrews and vertical drops. Consequently you are going to need something to cling to when approaching the scary bits or facing those feelings of regret. That is when you find yourself thinking "whatever possessed me to get on this ride in the first place?". The thing that you cling to is the initial passion you felt, the motivation and drive that compelled you to get started. Remember the feelings of excitement and invincibility that you have now and hold onto them. They will be your lifeline.

When I started in business, I had no previous business experience. I think this made me more willing to try new things because I didn't have lots of preconceived ideas of what one is supposed to do in business. I was able to build a really successful virtual assistant business very quickly because I paid attention to what was happening in the real world. Trends are great, but it's important to know the direction they are moving in. I saw a gap in the market and was able to exploit it because I was prepared to take the risk and trust my gut. Business is all about taking risks, being the first to try something new or repackage something in a different way. If you are only going to do what everyone else is doing, i.e. following the trend rather than follow your gut, you are going to have to compete on the same terms. As a newbie you may not have the connections, credibility in the market or the resources to push your way through. Find the path of least resistance and push against that rather than the fortified wall of competition. I've always followed my gut and taken the risks others weren't prepared to take. That's part of the reason I got into social media. I could see what a great tool it was and its potential, so whilst everyone else was busy jumping on the coaching bandwagon I started in social media. I am where I am today – I've been described as one of the most dynamic personalities in the UK social media market – because I followed my gut and took a risk on something that at that time people were saying was a fad for teenagers.

Today most of the old rules about being in business (if there were ever any hard and fast rules to begin with) need to be reassessed, particularly in terms of what is happening around you. It's back to being aware of your environment and paying attention. For example, everyone will tell you to find your niche. Whilst a niche is something to think about, if you are too tightly focused it makes it difficult to find customers. In today's market I believe the new entrepreneur has to think about a portfolio business. That is, being aware of the different segments of demand and opportunities to market new ranges of products to a wider audience.

Another thing that has changed dramatically is networking. You're going to hear a lot about how important it is to network and make connections. When I started my first business in 2006, networking was a relatively new concept to the mass market (those in the know had been networking for years) and so it was very easy to find networking groups and make great contacts. Unfortunately, networking was taken over by commercial interests and nowadays paid networking offers little if any advantages to the new entrepreneur because it is full of people who are looking to make sales. Networking is still as important for growing your business, however, you have to be a lot more savvy about how to use it.

The best way is to view networking is as a long-term investment in both yourself and your business. In other words, networking is about being able to make long lasting connections with people who will eventually become your advocates and supporters. The biggest mistake new entrepreneurs make is to believe that networking is about selling in the room. It is true that networking can find customers and therefore help your sales figures, however this normally happens through secondary connections and beyond.

The best place to start with networking is with your own personal networks. Ask people that already know and trust you to help you find business connections that will help you grow your business and solve issues rather then ask for sales. That way you will keep your friends and they will be willing to help you; rather than becoming the person that everybody wants to avoid because you're always trying to flog them something! Think of what you need to improve your business rather than what you want to sell.

In my first business, AskLilach, I networked like crazy. Very soon I had many clients lined up, indeed in the first two weeks of business I signed up ten clients just by using this strategy to network. I'm not saying that it will be this fast all the time, but when people understand you and what you can offer they refer others to you. So my advice is to use paid networks with caution, they can be huge time wasters; think of networking as creating friends who are your supporters and advocates.

Lilach Bullock

www.socialable.co.uk

Lilach is a business owner, social media consultant, internet mentor and founder of Socialable. One of the most dynamic personalities in the UK social media market, she actively leverages ethical internet marketing for her own and her clients' advantage.

Sole Trader Websites

Dear Entrepreneur,

Our Story

HISTORICALLY THE TILING BUSINESS had done very well from its advert in the local directory, but in the last five years Sebastian's father noticed that calls were drying up and when the UK recession began to bite in 2009, he was left with no alternative but to try and promote his business in other ways.

Sebastian realised his father's business (Mike Pollitt Tiling Specialist) had absolutely no web presence and there was a reason for this. Two years ago his father had tried to organise a very basic website but had found that every company providing web design or web building services could only offer a bespoke solution – an extremely costly option and normally one that was much more complicated than he required. This raised the second problem; Sebastian's father didn't use a computer and had little knowledge of how the internet and websites worked. When he approached a number of website builders with his requirements, he was constantly pointed to the internet where he was told he could build a website of his own. Knowing that this wasn't possible for him, he gave up and had since suffered as his competitors had gone online and seen the benefits from it.

It was this frustration that proved to be the breakthrough. After checking the Companies House database and numerous sole trader forums, Sebastian quickly discovered thousands of small businesses and sole traders in the UK that hadn't yet made the jump online and found that the cause was the same frustrations his father had been facing.

The solution to all these problems was the formation of Sole Trader Websites – a website builder that was born from the point of view of the customer and wouldn't forget its roots.

Today, it is committed to getting sole traders and small to medium-sized businesses their own website quickly, simply, cost-effectively and, unlike its competitors, provides its services 'offline' by offering a postal, fax and telephone service as well its online service.

Facts and Figures from Crowdcube

- Successfully raised £100k for 33% equity in 13 days to fund future growth.

- Sole Trader Websites also gained valuable input from an experienced investor who is now a non-executive director.

- One of Sole Trader Websites' greatest strengths is its pricing model that gives entry level sole traders the opportunity to have a website for their business.

- Sole Trader Websites needed its investment to grow its telesales team, further develop its own website and also to improve systems' administration processes.

- In the next three years Sole Trader Websites aims to have pre-tax revenues of £1.1 million.

- Founder and CEO, Sebastian Lewis', previous experience was as a stock broker with experience in options and equity derivatives.

My thoughts from my first year in business

1. First and foremost it is the hardest job you will ever have but the most rewarding when it goes well.

2. Always stick to your original plan and target market – if it's originally a good idea then it always will be. Plan, plan, plan and stick to it.

3. Don't be afraid of people telling you, you are mad and making a mistake – those people tend to stay in the same job for 30 years.

4. It helps to have personal experience with your 'typical customer' – my dad is a sole trader and I know how he ticks and what he needs, so I picture him in every business decision.

5. Don't be scared to take on the big established players…being small and nimble is an advantage.

66 **Plan, plan, plan and stick to it.** 99

Sebastian Lewis

Founder, Sole Trader Websites
www.soletraderwebsites.com

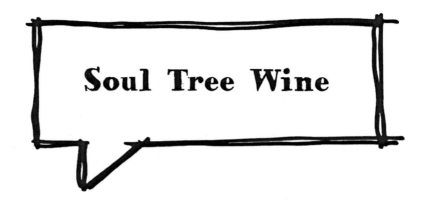

Soul Tree Wine

Dear Entrepreneur,

Y OU HAVE SET OUT ON THIS AMAZING ROLLER COASTER of a ride (believe me if it hasn't been one yet, it soon will be!) but you are probably well aware that success is far from guaranteed. In fact, statistically, success is outright elusive! So, if one can't guarantee success, how does one maximise the odds? Here are some practical aspects – some that we got bang on in our own start up and some not so much.

Get the right team!

Whether it is a team of two or of twenty in the early stages of your business, having the right team is one of the most important ingredients to success. The best ideas can flounder without the best team of people who share a common passion and vision, who bring a multitude of complementary skills to the business, and who can lift one another up in difficult times.

Know your core business!

How well do you know your core business? How much do you focus on it? As an entrepreneur you are probably full of ideas that keep on coming well after you have set the business wheels in motion. A successful entrepreneur, however, separates the wheat from the chaff and focuses on those ideas that help the core cause and discards those, however bright and appealing they may seem, that do not directly contribute to the core business.

Find a mentor!

Unless you have years and years of experience in your field (but even if you do), you should always look to someone with more relevant experience to help and guide you through the inevitable minefield of challenges. Even presidents and prime ministers have teams of advisors helping them! If nothing else, it pays huge dividends to have a sounding board – someone you can really trust and someone who can challenge or endorse your ideas and plans.

Do not overestimate the commercial potential behind the idea!

Sure, a fundamental part of starting up a new business is dreaming big. Huge success stories provide further fodder for the dreams and the ambitions, but a successful entrepreneur is a dreamer and a realist. Do not assume that you are destined for greatness just because someone else has successfully done something similar before. If you do not have a good vision of your strengths, competitive advantage, and of how you will carry your business to greatness, get back to the drawing board.

Believe in yourself!

Entrepreneurs are typically confident, but do you know if you have enough self-belief to carry you through the challenges that running a start-up enterprise will throw at you? Thousands of businesses start with supreme confidence but falter (and even fold) when tough times roll in and the whole world seems to turn against them. Successful entrepreneurs have self-belief in the bucket-loads and do not let challenges, however major they may seem at the time, to weigh them down. Sometimes the difference between success and failure is simply a matter of courage of conviction and of not giving up!

Plan for a long journey!

Each year thousands of new businesses fold up early in spite of a sound business plan. Amongst other reasons this is because, firstly, they underestimate the time-to-success and secondly, because they did not plan for the resources required to take the business through that extended period. It is critically important to realise that unless you are a one-in-a-million tech industry start-up, the road to success is usually a long one, and that a business needs time and resources to function and succeed. One cannot plan for everything and if one tried perhaps a venture would never take off, but successful entrepreneurs anticipate and plan for extended periods of resource challenges, net losses and crippling cash flow crunches.

Cash is king!

A cliché, but certainly no overstatement! Profitability is great, but not the measure you should worry about in the early years of your venture. A business can trade, and survive, without profits, but will fold in a flash without the cash to pay suppliers, service providers, and employees. Equally, the availability of liquid funds could be one of the most important factors in enabling growth. Successful entrepreneurs plan well for cash flow and always keep one eye on it.

Be willing to learn!

The biggest asset an entrepreneur can have is the willingness to learn. Successful entrepreneurs have supreme confidence in themselves and in what they do, but they are also always open to new ideas, to challenge and be challenged, and to change and adapt. Flexible and nimble businesses that are best able to adapt to changing consumer needs and market situations have the best odds of making it big.

Fervent passion for the cause, or grounded feet?

Both, in equal measure! The business probably would not even start if one does not have the passion to put in the extraordinary effort required to start up, or to take the risk. But passion alone will only get you so far. Too driven by the dream? Find a business partner or associate to manage the business or you could end up with broken dreams. Too sensible and grounded? Find a business partner or associate who can continually dream the dreams that will take provide your business with the reach-the-sky ambitions.

Which brings us, full circle, to the top of this list – have the right team!

Best wishes!

Alok Mathur & Melvin D'Souza

Founders, Soul Tree Wine
Putting Indian Wine on the Map!
www.soultreewine.co.uk

Dear Entrepreneur,

CONGRATULATIONS! IF YOU'VE PICKED UP THIS BOOK, it's probably because you have a feeling there's a business in you. That doesn't happen to everyone. It's a special thing, and you should know that. If you're already actively thinking about that business idea, even better. Get excited. There's a big adventure ahead. Lucky you!

Here are my top 3 tips for you, from my journey so far:

1. Love your idea, keep it loose, and get obsessed

If you're right, and this idea really is as great as you think it is, you're probably going to be working on it day and night for the next few years. You're going to need to stay happy and stay excited by it for a long time. So you better choose the right one!

Do this by spending time with it, get to know it properly, eat with it, shower with it, sleep with it :) Be patient with it and let it change, adapt and evolve, let it grow and surprise you.

When I started out inventing sugru, I had no idea it would take so many years, or be so difficult. I had a vision for it as a kind of space-age rubber that anyone could use to repair and modify almost anything. I imagined it as super easy to shape, sticky, and durable. I knew it needed to feel gorgeous and that, if I cracked it, it'd have a million uses.

Making that vision real turned out to be super tough though. I had to get into the world of material science (one I was new to), convince amazing scientists and investors to come onboard, learn how to be a lab technician and put the hours in the lab for several years. Later it involved pitching to large companies, taking the plunge to launch our own brand, establishing our own factory and employing a growing number of people.

Nine years since my initial idea, I still feel thrilled by the same simple vision I had at the start. Helping the world to get repairing again is a mission I feel very deeply, somewhere in my tummy, and it feeds off my urge to help create the kind of world I want to be part of. The effect that this business can have means much more than making a living, that's only a means to an end – the thing that's brought me through the huge highs and lows over the years is the potential to make a positive change in the world.

2.   Work with people who're excited to make this happen

One of the lessons I learned fastest was that you can't do everything yourself. There are amazing people out there who are fantastic at 'their thing', whether that's science, engineering, web design or sales – make sure you involve them. If at the beginning you can't afford to pay these people, get their input and advice at least, or find alternative ways of paying them if it makes sense. Early on, I teamed up with my business partner Roger, who has a lifetime's experience in business, something I had no experience of whatsoever. But it wasn't just his business experience that made him the right choice of partner; when we talked about sugru and my vision for it, his eyes lit up. He regularly used the prototypes. And he worked hard to gain my trust and help me make progress. He didn't act like an expert, he supported me to do it. Those are the things that sealed the deal.

2.   Start small and make it good

Sometimes, we get so seduced with the idea of something being big, that we forget what's really important. The most important thing is that it's right. If it's right and it gets ten people excited, and they have a great user experience, and they need it again or recommend it, you can grow to 100 people. From there you can grow to 1000, 10,000, 1m and beyond. If it's not right for ten, you'll learn why and you'll make it right. Start small and make it good!

And just as a last note, in a book full of advice – it's cool that you're looking to learn from people who've been there. You can learn lots that way. But don't forget... they may not be right. No matter who they are or how much experience they have, people often apply old rules to new ideas.

They've never been you, doing this idea, in this time.

Listen to them, think about it, and then go with your gut.

And, remember, have fun!

JaneNí Dhulchaointigh

Founder, Sugru
www.sugru.com

Dear Entrepreneur,

HERE ARE SOME POINTERS THAT MIGHT hopefully be useful:

Research - Questions to yourself

You need to ask yourself the right questions. If they're the right questions then you won't know the answers to all of them. Some common ones might be about how your business will differ from competitors, who your customers might be, why they would choose to buy from you, how much money you will need, where you might get it from and so on. Speaking to friends and family might help generate the list of questions, but then you need to gather brutally honest answers.

Fill in the gaps in information by any means you can – speak to as many people as possible, use the internet, trade journals, magazines – whatever you can use. A crucial part of this is identifying and understanding your USP or unique selling point, which I believe to be the bedrock of any business. So many would-be entrepreneurs don't understand the importance of this – make sure you aren't one of them. Gaining investment and sales will often depend upon this as a major factor.

Resilience

You will need patience and mental toughness in your toolkit because things never quite go to plan. In fact, you could help yourself by always building extra into your plan – extra time, extra money, etc. If your idea is good and there is a market for it you will find the funding you need, you will persuade the right suppliers to help you and you will sell it to the customers, but each of these steps can involve quite a few knock backs and you need to be able to pick yourself up and carry on regardless. This is not a short journey and it isn't one for the faint hearted.

Suppliers

Businesses flourish on strong trading relationships and this isn't just true in the case of your customers. Your suppliers are just as important. There can be a false assumption that all suppliers will be glad of new business, but this is only true to a point. The investment required in time and other resources mean that in certain industries, suppliers have their pick of who to deal with. When the time comes convince them that you're a good proposition by knowing the answers to all those questions I just mentioned. Also, make sure you speak to them the 'right' way. Confidence is good. Going in like you know it all from day one isn't. An experienced supplier can be a great source of information, advice and support. They know their industry inside out and that probably means that they know your industry inside out. Respect them and always be honest with them, whether the news is good or bad. You will find in time that this is what you hope for from your customers too.

> **" Confidence is good. Going in like you know it all from day one isn't. "**

Work ON your business

It is easy to create yourself a job and work in your business, but for real growth you need to work **on** your business. By this I mean you need to look at your strategy and your plans for growth, not just your job list for the day. One way to help with this is to outsource where possible. We outsource the manufacture of our drinks and concentrate on driving distribution and building brand equity. This gives us flexibility for growth and the clarity of mind to focus on core goals for the business.

Have a life

It is easy to be consumed by your work and there will certainly be plenty to do. Make sure you maintain a healthy work-life balance. Try to switch off at times. See your friends and family. Have fun. Life is not all about work and remembering this will probably actually help your business by maintaining a sense of perspective.

Health

Your physical health is important. Looking after yourself will help you stay energised, benefit your mental health and contribute to self-confidence, which are all important for entrepreneurs.

I hope these points are of some help. If anyone has any specific questions, you can contact me via the SUMO website or on LinkedIn.

Best of luck,

Richard

Creator and MD, SUMO
www.sumodrinks.com

SuperJam

STARTING A BUSINESS MIGHT CHANGE YOUR LIFE (and maybe even the world!).

As I kid, I was always fascinated by the possibility of making my life into whatever I wanted it to be, by starting my own business, creating something from nothing and taking my destiny into my own hands.

For me, starting a business has never been about trying to get rich. I've never had fantasies of living in a mansion, holidaying on a yacht or anything of the sort. For me, I have always loved the feeling that comes from creating something. There is nothing more amazing than the feeling of someone paying his or her hard-earned money to buy something you have created. Their money validates that you created something worthwhile.

My adventures in entrepreneurship began at perhaps what was an unusually young age. Even as a small boy, I was coming up with ideas to try to make a bit of extra pocket money. But in fact, whatever money I made when I was eight or nine years old, I sent to my favourite charity, which at the time was Greenpeace. My Mum has all these letters that she kept; "Dear Mr. Doherty, thank you for your donation of £4.50".

By the time I got to my teens, I couldn't quite figure out how running a business could have an effect on some of the wider social issues that I felt strongly about. At least until I read about the stories of Ben & Jerry's,

The Body Shop, Patagonia and some other socially-minded companies. They proved that it was possible to run a commercially successful business in a way that also has a social and environmental benefit.

Inspired by these stories, I went on to start SuperJam at the age of fourteen, in my Gran's tiny kitchen in Glasgow. I started out by making a few dozen jars of jam at a time, selling them at farmers' markets and to small shops. A couple of years later, I had developed an all-natural way of making jam 100% from fruit, moved production into a factory and created a brand.

Since then, we have sold many millions of jars of SuperJam through close to 2,000 supermarket stores in eight countries around the world. The brand has gone on to win over twenty awards and was even entered into the National Museum of Scotland as an example of an iconic Scottish brand!

One of the things that I am most proud of is the fact that SuperJam has been able to invest some of its profits into doing good in our community. We have run many hundreds of free SuperJam tea parties for elderly people who live alone or in care. We put on live music, dancing and scones and jam – really just giving the elderly people a chance to get out of the house, have a bit of fun and maybe a dance.

Something I have been amazed by on my journey has been how willing other entrepreneurs have been willing to share their lessons, mistakes and advice with me. I've learned all kinds of things, but if I was to share my top three pieces of advice they would be to: Start small, ask for help, and just not to be afraid.

I think a lot of people imagine that they have to jump in at the deep end, quit their job and borrow a whole bunch of money to get their idea off the ground. I don't think that is true; it's possible to dip your toe into the water by starting something in the weekends and evenings after school or work. Once you've had some small successes, it'll give you the confidence to invest more into your idea.

Probably the best help and support I got was from having a mentor, a guy called Kevin. He had set up a successful business supplying supermarkets and was just willing to share some of the lessons he had learned along the way. I can highly recommend finding someone who has been there and done it before to ask for advice.

Finally, I meet a huge number of people who dream of starting a business. Some of them even have an idea. But, most people are too afraid of taking the first steps and giving their ideas a shot. They worry that people might laugh at them, that the business will go bust or that nobody will believe in them. In reality, you have so much less to lose than you imagine from just trying.

> **❝ I can highly recommend finding someone who has been there and done it before to ask for advice. ❞**

So, I guess perhaps what my story shows is that something that can begin for anyone as a hobby or a passion in a kitchen, a bedroom, a garage or even a garden shed, can grow into something amazing, something that changes your life. I know that SuperJam has certainly changed mine. Something that gives you a career and, hopefully, an opportunity to give something back to your community.

I wish you the best of luck on your adventure!

Fraser Doherty

Founder, SuperJam
www.fraserdoherty.com

SuperJam™

SuperTie

Dear Entrepreneur,

WHEN I STARTED SUPERTIE and Chris Gibson Design, I was very much a business rookie.

Having trained as a lawyer, I took the jump into the world of the entrepreneur. It is one of the best decisions I have ever made. Even though I had no academic training in anything specifically business orientated, the last three years or so have effectively been a practical degree in creating and then running a business. I have come to learn that being an entrepreneur and managing a business is a lifestyle choice. It's different and seriously challenging, but also an exciting way to experience life for a certain type of person.

All entrepreneurs will pick out certain principles or mantras that they hold dear in how they and their ideas have developed. These can be quite personal, wide-ranging and varied. Here are my top five:

1. What is your vision?

Where do you want to get to with your idea? Think hard about what you want to achieve – where does your passion lie? When you work that out, that gives you a main goal and a main focus. Everything you go on to do, should then be about pursuing that vision. As human beings, we operate much better when we have a self-made target or goal. The trick then, is to reach that long-term target. If you have no target, then how can you aim?

2. You are your business

It seems like stating the obvious to say it, but sometimes this simplest of doctrines needs to be properly emphasised. This principle can pass you by when you're a business rookie with so many things to consider. It took me three years to fully comprehend it. Think of Richard Branson and Virgin. Virgin is Richard Branson. The name Virgin was bold and challenging, just like Sir Richard. If you study Virgin, you'll see that most of what you know Virgin to be as a brand closely reflects the person behind it. When you start a business, the architect of that business is you. You create it, nurture and develop it. It is a reflection of your own personality and energies. The business then develops a personality that people relate to and connect with or become aware of. That personality is your business's brand.

3. Engage with people. Listen, learn, analyse and evaluate

One of the best things about being an entrepreneur is discovering how much you can learn from other people. Not just business people, but everyone. Your customers, the public, a CEO, a designer, your doctor, your parents, your friends – the list is endless. They all have insights, ideas and information that can possibly directly help you, but very importantly, will always indirectly help you. This is because they have experiences and knowledge that will add to yours when shared. That shared information can help you analyse and evaluate how to achieve your visions. Talk to people. Learn from them. I've yet to meet anybody who doesn't have a story to tell, or information to share, that hasn't been useful in some way, no matter how slight.

4. Trial and error

I learned the most from the mistakes I made, or the things that went wrong. If you can identify a problem, and then fix it, that is invaluable. At every opportunity you attempt to sell your product or service, whether successful or unsuccessful, always look to see what could be done better, or what could be done to make it successful. The answers will be there, but you must work hard and think hard in order to find them.

5. The master of your own destiny

Despite all the risks and concerns that come with starting out on your own, it can be immensely empowering and liberating. Perhaps not with your body and time in the early days (due to inevitable periods of hard work) but always with your mind and soul. Stress, strain, worry and pain are all there in abundance, just like in most careers, but the difference is, you are working for yourself. As such, this better empowers you as the master of your own destiny.

Oh, and finally, I think we all make most of our own luck. But good luck anyway!

Chris Gibson

Founder, SuperTie
www.supertie.com

Andy Sutton

Dear Entrepreneur,

Buckle up and enjoy the ride – the rewards take care of themselves

BEING AN ENTREPRENEUR IS not for the faint-hearted but for those that take the plunge, the rewards are almost always, enormous. I am sure that most people reading this will equate the word reward to 'money' but in this context nothing could be further from the truth. Of course, the potential for significant financial reward is why most people are attracted to the 'entrepreneur' label but achieving this ultimate outcome is by no means certain. In contrast, I can confidently predict that the fantastic rewards you receive in other areas will come, by default, whether your venture is successful or not.

Having spent six years at university studying engineering, I spent the next 17 years working in a large corporate environment using none of the engineering skills I'd spent six years learning! Over many years, I enjoyed considerable success and climbed the corporate ladder to a very senior role in the IT industry. This was a fast-paced, albeit comfortable, existence where I got paid (a lot) at the end of every month and played my small part in the engine of a well-oiled corporate machine. It was challenging at times (sales targets had to be hit) but looking back, one day looked pretty much the same as the next. Perhaps the most frustrating aspect of corporate life was that the opportunity to think 'off-piste' was rare and was almost always quashed at source. All too late, I realised that I was being successful but in an environment of people who liked the status quo and were prepared to work hard doing largely the same things every day. Do I really want to do this for another 20 years I asked myself? The answer was simple. Stepping out of that corporate 'grind' was a straightforward decision and one that I wish I had taken sooner. I have now been an entrepreneur for over seven years and during that period I have developed, learned and experienced so much more than in all my prior working life. But the entrepreneur's road is a rocky one and it should only be contemplated if you have a cast-iron will to succeed, boundless energy and enthusiasm, a thick skin (a fear of rejection is not something that should be high on your list of weaknesses!) and the ability to focus unerringly on your goals. Forget the monthly pay cheque, forget the comfortable existence and embrace the raw realities of growing a business.

The rewards for an entrepreneur extend far beyond the destination, which if you are talented, dogged, resourceful, and to some extent lucky, might eventually result in the pot of gold you dream about. Of more significance perhaps are the rewards of experience, insight and knowledge you undoubtedly glean on the way. You can read all the theory in the world, engross yourself in an MBA and still come nowhere near to the benefits of being out there, running a business, making mistakes (and learning from them), finding solutions and navigating success.

It is no surprise that many of the world's most successful business leaders come from humble beginnings, having taken an entrepreneurial track in early life and learning the hard way. Being an entrepreneur isn't for most people and if you have to think too hard about it, it probably isn't for you. But if you have that fire in your belly, are prepared to greet those two imposters, success and failure, just the same and have an unstinting appetite for success, then grasp the nettle and make a difference. The rewards will take care of themselves and you might just hit that pot of gold.

Andy Sutton

Founder & Chief Executive,
Bag That Trading Ltd

Starting up

IWAS HAPPY BUT LONELY IN MY NEW ROLE as a mum. I'd always worked hard and despite being the best mother I could be, a little bit of me wasn't there anymore. I realised I needed to do something, something that would ultimately help people and make life easier.

Being a first-time mum I realised just how much stuff you accumulate, along with the additional pressure of having to pay for it all, that was when ToyBoxLive came to life. I realised that I couldn't be the only parent who wanted their child to learn through play, but what I was seeing was how quickly both myself and my daughter needed new experiences and toys to use to help each other learn. My own toy spending was getting out of hand and my house was quickly being taken over with unused and unloved toys that were still in pristine condition; something had to be done. Surely I couldn't be the only parent to feel this way, it was then that the idea of renting toys rather than buying them came to me.

Despite toy libraries being commonplace in most towns I found them to be hard to access and the quality of the toys didn't match my own expectations. That's when I decided ToyBoxLive would be the UK's first online toy library. Imagining a service that wasn't geographically confined, where parents or carers could access toys from an online company operating in the 21st century, with quality and value at the heart of it.

The first part was research: was anyone else offering this type of service and how were they doing it? There was nobody in the UK offering an online toy rental service and with the growth of rental services in the entertainment and software markets it was a no brainer that I had to give it a go.

I set up ToyBoxLive as a limited company on the 1st June 2010, and I steadily worked on the idea over the next six months, researching products, consumer behaviour and costs.

ToyBoxLive.co.uk had its official launch on 23rd December 2010, where we did a charity drop of presents to the children who would be in hospital over Christmas, I then drastically rushed to get a press release out but unfortunately with it being around Christmas time it wasn't very well received.

The next few months included constant marketing and updating the website. I also set up my blog (**www.toy-rental.co.uk**), where I review products and what is going on in the toy market. I then set up Twitter and Facebook accounts and really started pushing everything, as well as perfecting our elevator pitch: "the UK's first online toy rental service".

Setting up in business isn't for everyone, you have to be prepared to put in the work, but the rewards and personal satisfaction are worth it.

Alison Chesworth

Founder, ToyBoxLive
www.toyboxlive.co.uk

Trifle Creative*

Dear Entrepreneur,

I DON'T SEE MYSELF AS A TRADITIONAL ENTREPRENEUR. I never set out to run a huge business empire and that's not what I do. I have a small business which is not focussed on only making money, the motivator for me was about having the freedom to do what I love, to create and push creative boundaries, to mix with people from all walks of life and make their lives better or more interesting in some way and to never, ever have to do the same thing day after day.

It took me a while to work out what I wanted to do exactly, and I did that by freelancing and dipping a toe in here and there. Creative enlightenment came to me courtesy of ?What If! Innovation where I worked for five years in my early 20s. I started as a junior but had a great passion for the work and the culture and as such was allowed a lot of freedom to step up and take on bigger roles and get involved in many parts of the business. This gave me the confidence to recognise where my talents did lie (and where they didn't).

From an early age I was more of a 'dress the space' kind of girl than a 'dress up' girl. I think my Mum still regrets the year she said I could do what I wanted to the house for a huge New Year's Eve party she was throwing...I sourced 8 kilos of glitter and sprinkled the entire house, driveway absolutely everywhere with it. Two years later she was still finding glitter. For me, transforming spaces and making them more interesting, exciting, engaging and magical was always the thing I loved doing. I used the natural abilities I had in many ways before I honed in on commercial interior design. I am absolutely passionate about what I do and you have to be to run your own business because it is unbelievably hard work, you live and breathe it, and if you don't love it then move on and find the thing you do. We spend the majority of our adult waking lives at work and you need to be incredibly driven and self-motivated to really make it happen.

Be organised

Start off with simple systems and ways of keeping yourself organised in the early days (files, systems, IT backing up and storage, receipts, accounts, research and sourcing) and this will really help you as your business grows. As a visual business we are big fans of Evernote and Pinterest and have no idea where we'd be without Dropbox. Find what's right for you and get into good habits early on. Get help and support where you need to by talking to friends and using brilliant free sources like Business Link.

Keep your finger on the pulse

Whether it's trade shows, relevant press and media, people you follow on Twitter, etc. keep on top of news and trends relevant to you and your industry. Once in a while take time to get out and about. This will keep you in the know and stimulated. Many an idea has been sparked for us by walking around the Tate Modern or window browsing at Selfridges. Where and what keeps your brain energised and stimulated? Make sure you know before you start as it is going to need recharging, frequently, once you get stuck into your new business.

Get skilled up

Surround yourself with all the necessary skills by either:

- learning them, or

- sourcing people that have them who can work on a freelance basis.

You can't do everything so make sure you have people around you that can. Have honest conversations with everyone you know about what you want to do, you never know what skills you will uncover right under your nose. PeoplePerHour has been a brilliant resource for us in this respect. The reality is you cannot possibly learn and know everything but do as much as you can in the early days, as this will give you confidence. When you don't know the critical stuff pause and find out, don't guess in areas you really don't know anything about but at the same time don't be fearful of being in at the deep end.

Think about where you work

Of course it depends what kind of business you are starting but don't think you need to rush out and get an office. See what space you have at home to make into a great working space. Think about what kind of work you need to do, how can it inspire you, keep you productive and energised and also allow you quiet thinking working time. You need different types of space for different types of work or simple ways of keeping your space flexible so that it can work for you and enhance what you're doing, not hinder. Therefore it's equally important to recognise when you do need more space. My first desk was in a dark hallway – it was great for storage and I could surround myself with all the resource books and inspiring magazines and other things – but I quickly realised the lack of natural light was prohibitive to long working days! I ear-marked local and further afield coffee shops I could work in, hotels are particularly great for this. The Hoxton Hotel was particularly good as I could easily and comfortably work as well as hold meetings there in a fantastic environment. Developing our loft into a home office space allowed me to grow the business further.

Think about who you work with

Having a great team and great suppliers has been critical to my business. Building working relationships within my friendship network has really worked for me and gives our projects a "family feel". Building relationships with people I wouldn't usually hang out with has been equally essential and it is really important to nurture those working relationships and look after people that do great work for the business.

Get accounts savvy

Getting a C in GCSE maths was hard work for me so when I started managing lengthy budgets and trying to understand what I needed to charge in order to make the business work, I really had to work hard at it. Learning the Excel basics has been essential but so has recognising my weaknesses around this area and using people who know how. Having a bookkeeper is the singularly most important thing you can do unless you are able to do this yourself. We essentially ran our business 'blind' for a while and the combination of this and an accountant that gave little advice meant we had huge problems with our accounts. Having a decent accountant and bookkeeper is critical. We use KashFlow now and I only wish we had done so from the start.

5 things a day which could lead to a sale

I have to thank Naked Wines who won the Smarta award the year we were runners up for this one, but ever since they stated their mantra we have adapted it for ourselves and aim to do three of the following every day:

1. Tweet

2. Update your blog

3. Highlight a potential client or new market and cold call or email them

4. Contact an old client and find out what's going on in their world

5. Research what's going on in your industry and see if there are any governing bodies you can be involved with

6. Find a trade show coming up, book onto it and create some clever new business cards especially to hand out

7. Update your Facebook page

8. Create/update Pinterest – Hunt around to see if anything relevant is going on you can tap into and anything you can bring in visually to the Pinterest community

Use failures as a stepping stone

Mistakes will happen, and things will go wrong, it's inevitable but it's how you handle them that can make or break. I have always tried to be an optimist, to turn failures into learnings; use them to make you better and to make you grow, use them as stepping stones to future success.

Emma Morley
Founder, Trifle Creative*
www.triflecreative.com

Turtle Tots

Dear Future Entrepreneur,

STARTING A NEW BUSINESS IS A HUGE, LIFE-CHANGING, exciting and terrifying thing to do! It can also be incredibly satisfying, rewarding and fun!

We founded Turtle Tots in 2011. Gaby and I both have corporate backgrounds but after we had children we started our own businesses:

- Gaby was one of the first franchisees for a well-known baby swimming company and ran the Oxfordshire and Berkshire franchises for four years, teaching over 1000 babies a week with a team of teachers and administrators. In 2008 Gaby sold the franchises for 15 times what she had paid for them, and moved to Bristol with her young family.

- Caroline worked for Virgin Media in various marketing and communications roles for 12 years. After having her second child she wanted a more flexible job and started her own exhibition business called Little Monster. For five years Caroline organised baby and toddler exhibitions across the South West. Each exhibition attracted around 60 exhibitors and over 1000 visitors but after five years Caroline needed a new challenge and having decided to sell Little Monster last year, was approached by Gaby about launching Turtle Tots Ltd. Caroline was able to sell her Little Monster business quickly and join Gaby.

Our brief histories above illustrate something that people don't often consider when they start their business – that they are creating an asset that will grow in value as their business grows!

At Turtle Tots we sell licences to people who want to run their own Turtle Tots swimming businesses. At the time of writing we have 15 licencees and each licencee has their own reasons for taking the leap of becoming a business owner and entrepreneur.

The most common reason we hear is flexibility. Running your own business allows you to set your own hours, and work from wherever you want. With today's technology it's perfectly feasible to work wirelessly from almost anywhere! Many of our licencees have young children and don't want to return to their 9-5 jobs and incur huge nursery fees – by running their own business they can work around their children and avoid childcare costs.

Our licencees also want the opportunity to grow something that will reward them – both mentally and financially. When you run your own business there's no ceiling to what you can earn. It's incredibly exciting and a fantastic feeling to know that the effort you put in can directly influence the financial growth of your business.

Of course there's all the planning and practical stuff to consider too. There's always an element of risk when you start a business, but the more planning and research you do upfront, the more the risk is mitigated. Writing a detailed business plan is a "must do"; whether or not you need to borrow money to start your business. But don't leave it to gather dust; review it regularly to ensure you are meeting your targets and objectives.

Put processes in place to cope with your workload as you grow – otherwise you'll be chasing your own tail. And put a value on your own time. It's very easy to spend time on jobs which would be far better to be done by someone else; allowing you to concentrate on what you're best at.

We could carry on and on talking about the advantages of starting a business – but perhaps the best advice is don't keep talking (or reading) about it – JUST DO IT!

Caroline Spark

Founder, Turtle Tots
www.turtletots.com

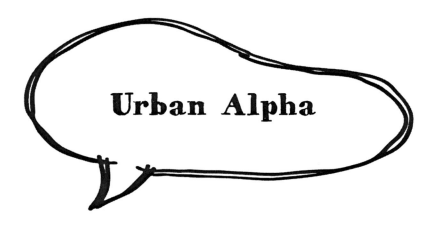

Urban Alpha

I WAS A RELATIVE LATECOMER TO entrepreneurialism –
I didn't start selling sweets at school and I wasn't an
enterprising youth with three paper rounds (I did not
and still do not like early mornings) – but I've always
been very creative.

I'd always be drawing or taking things apart to learn how they worked,
and that has helped me spot opportunities and come up with creative
ways to 'solve the problem'. One such example that no one believes is
that, as an 11-year-old boy, I invented Moonpig. Well, the concept of
Moonpig anyway. It's a long story, but ultimately I ended up not going
through with it. Partly because my business partner (my Uncle David)
wanted 51% equity and I refused to budge, but mainly because I afraid
of what would happen if I failed.

Would people think I was stupid? Would they make fun of me? What if
I lost all my money? How would I pay the money back? Perhaps not the
questions I asked myself then, but they were questions that had held back
a number of my business ideas. Maybe some of them would've worked,
maybe some of them wouldn't – I guess now I'll never know.

Anyway, after a lot more ideas, I finally had one that I thought was worth
pursuing. So I did my usual trick of writing business plans, coming up
with strategies, and as expected I hit the wall. What happens if it doesn't

work? How will I convince everyone to sell to me? This time, however, something was different.

I've had this written on a Post-it note on my bedroom wall for years:

"Entrepreneurship is the pursuit of opportunity without regard to resources currently controlled. "

That is a definition by Howard Stevenson, a professor at Harvard Business School. I read it every morning. Although the meaning changes every morning depending on the previous day's events or the current days objectives, the morning when I decided to commit to the business it meant 'don't be afraid of failure'.

One of the main things I've discovered from being in business as a young entrepreneur is that I don't know everything. I spend a lot of time reading books and talking with other entrepreneurs to learn as much as I can about ecommerce, but one of the best ways of learning has come from being in business because it forces you to learn. I now think to myself 'if I don't solve this problem, I could lose a sale' and 'if this doesn't work how it's supposed to, I might not get picked up properly by Google' which motivates me to solve problems and come up with creative solutions.

So if I had one piece of advice for a budding entrepreneur, it would be to go for it. Pure and simple. If it works first time, great. Pat yourself on the back. Job well done. If it doesn't, don't worry about it too much. Provided you learn from the experience, you should wear that failure like a badge of honour. Not everyone gets it right the first time, but I feel the sign of a true entrepreneur is the willingness to keep trying, to keep pursuing the opportunity, until you get it right.

Andrew Pallett

Founder, Urban Alpha
www.urbanalpha.co.uk

Urban Coffee Company

Dear Entrepreneur,

I WAS SAT IN A COOL, INDEPENDENT LONDON coffee shop with my now business partner brainstorming new ideas for a business when the conversation got around to the amazing coffee we were drinking and how it was really difficult to get good coffee in cities outside of London. That was the day Urban Coffee Company was born. Of course, it took lots more conversations, blood, sweat and tears before we were ready to sell our first coffee. Just to give you an idea, Urban Coffee Company is an off high street, high-end coffee retailer. In fact, we serve the best coffee this side of the moon, hand-crafted by our highly trained urbanistas (our version of a Barista).

Before we started, we spoke to lots of people both in the industry and your average coffee shop goer and the resounding message we got from them was that the market is crowded; oh no, not another coffee shop. The learning from that is, don't listen to everything you are told. If you have done your research (and you MUST do your research) and you are sure, then go for it – we did and haven't looked back since.

From day one we set out with the idea of making our staff one of our differentiators – we wanted them to be great with customers and known for being friendly. Now, you would think that is a given or easy to find – well, it's not. How many times have you been into a retail outlet and been ignored by a member of staff or just thought 'smile, for goodness sake'? Good people are the hardest thing to find and we spend a lot of time weeding out those who are not naturally friendly, who don't smile, who are not positive. We interview them, then bring them in for trial shifts and let the other urbanistas decide if they are a cultural fit or not – that way we don't just have a manager deciding but a whole bunch of people at all levels of the business. The other thing we do is hire for attitude and not skill; we can train people to make amazing coffee or to work on our accounts but we can't change people's attitude.

66 Don't listen to everything you are told 99

There is a saying that happy staff = happy customers = profit – guess what, it is true. So, you have to find a way to keep your staff happy and bought into the vision of the business. We have found this hard, particularly when the business is growing at a fast pace. People you hire when you only have one shop and five people will find the changes that are required to grow the business uncomfortable. For instance, with only five people you can just tell people we do things like this but when you have twenty people across multiple shops you have to write stuff into process documents and have more formal stuff. So you can expect to lose some of your early people because they like and are suited to the small startups culture; don't take it as a sign of failure, it's a sign of growth, growing pains if you will.

66 Hire slowly, be choosy but fire quickly. 99

If I had one bit of final advice for you, it would be to hire slowly, be choosy but fire quickly. If people turn out not to be the naturally friendly person you thought or aren't a great cultural fit, then it's in both parties' interest to part company quickly. This can feel uncomfortable, and often you will continue to make excuses for them or find reasons to put off firing them, but you should just get it done as soon as it becomes an issue.

Good luck with your adventure. Go knock their socks off with your idea.

Yours,

Simon

Americano, black no sugar

Co-founder, Urban Coffee Company
www.urbancoffee.co.uk

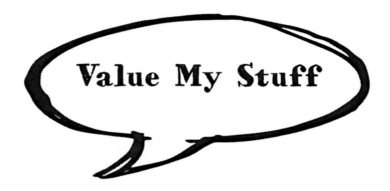

Value My Stuff

Dear Entrepreneur,

THANK YOU FOR TAKING THE TIME TO READ my letter. I am not sure what I can advise when starting up a business, apart from making sure you are hungry to do business, work very hard and be ready for the roller coaster ride! Setting up your own business has highs and lows: the highs mainly coming from seeing there is a need for your business idea and that customers are flowing in, taking up your services, and the lows mainly driven by financials, as things don't always go to plan, nor revenues don't always necessarily follow. That said, it is the most magnificent journey you embark upon, and you should enjoy every minute of it, as no day is ever the same, and every day brings new challenges and moments of doubt, moments of joy!

The main inspiration for setting up my own business was two-fold: on the one hand, I wanted to set a challenge for myself, to see how I would fare setting up my own business and having been inspired by business people over the years, I did have itchy feet to start my own business; the second, main component was that the enthusiasm for the actual business idea itself (once I had it clear in my mind what I wanted to do) drove me to take the plunge and go for it! What I wanted to do was to transform the art and antiques business, make it less elite, more accessible to all and very transparent. Whilst we are already halfway there, there is still a long way to go, which continues to drive me forward and push the business on all levels.

❝ If you can handle being shaken and stirred then go for it! ❞

I often get asked the question 'why didn't I stay at Sotheby's and continue to work for them after 13 years being there?'. That surely was a dream job? Oh yes it was: I did see great clients, lovely houses, beautiful estates, astonishing collections, helping organise sales for the likes of Elton John and Carla Bruni's mum, BUT after a while the novelty and challenge wears off. You become part of a routine. That routine which does appeal to many people, became quite numbing for me, and I did feel myself slipping away into a life where intellectually or emotionally I felt less challenged in the work environment. Now, however, things are almost too much the opposite way: great successes, great disappointments, no routine and 200% effort. So do think carefully about setting up your own business: if you can handle being shaken and stirred when setting up your own business, then go for it!

In a way I see the start of Value My Stuff as something that was meant to happen on my life journey and something I always worked towards even though I didn't quite know from the beginning. The idea sort of grew organically during my years at Sotheby's and crystallised at the

❝ Don't force yourself to reinvent the wheel; you will invent the wheel when you see the need for it! ❞

end. That is often a mistake I see: people want to set up their own business but are breaking their heads about what they can do, whereas they should set up, almost forcing themselves to come up with the newest novel idea. In my view, the more naturally the idea can grow out of something else you are doing, the better. Don't force yourself to reinvent the wheel; you will invent the wheel when you see the need for it!

Dear Entrepreneur, good luck on your journey, your path and remember, enjoy every minute of it, even when things are not easy for you. You will be out there on your own, taking your own decisions, making your own mistakes, but be assured, the reward is there at the end of it!

Patrick van der Vorst

Founder, Value My Stuff
www.valuemystuff.com

Wealthy Student

Dear Entrepreneur,

To START ANYTHING NEW IN LIFE REQUIRES motivation. It requires passion and a steadfast 'screw what you think, I am doing this. I'm doing this for me and nobody is going to stop me'.

This is how I started. I was at university in Southampton and had a part-time job selling cruise holidays (which paid quite well for a student). I was the best sales person they had but when it came round for my yearly review the guy who owned the company wouldn't give me a 50p per hour pay rise. Needless to say, I thought it was a joke. I immediately resigned and started my own company, **Wealthystudent.co.uk** – a site designed to help students save money at university.

I was also driven by the intense desire to design my own life, live where I wanted and not be governed by the 9 to 5 paradigm in which the majority of the population live.

This was over four years ago and there has been a lot of ups and downs along the way and I'm still fighting my way up to the top.

My top tips for anyone starting out would be:

1. Spend as little money as possible to test your idea. You don't need to spend mega bucks to see if your idea works. The absolute MAXIMUM you should spend is £1000 or perhaps £1500 to get started. You can get a website done for £300. Don't spend the £10,000 I once did and suffer afterwards.

2. Start as early as possible when you get an idea, do not wait around for tomorrow to come. University is an ideal place to start a business as you don't have the burden of a full-time job. Even if the business doesn't work, a future employer (if you have to work for a bit after university, as I did – but only for six months) will see you as an exemplary candidate for the fact you tried something.

3. Get a support group. Your friends will probably think you are crazy for starting a business, I think I had one friend who supported me at the beginning. Most of your friends don't want to see you fail so they won't back you but there are plenty of people outside your normal social circle who will help. Get to business networking groups on LinkedIn or Meetup. Finding a support network to bounce ideas off is invaluable when you first start out.

4. Enter competitions once you get started. I entered a few and you get recognition. Securing *Men's Health* Magazine's Entrepreneur of the Year helped me to get new business and find new opportunities. Also joining the Courvoisier Future 500 Network has helped me find some great friends and business contacts.

5. Do not be fooled into thinking that you can do this alone, you can't. Nobody in this world who achieved anything of worth did it alone, you need help. Do not be scared to reach out for help or to go looking for a business partner. Going through starting up a business on your own is incredibly tough. This goes beyond your support group as you are going to need people helping you with the business day in, day out.

Above all, just get going. Put one foot in front of the other and in a few days, weeks and months time you will thank yourself so much.

Good luck!

Steve Burford

Founder, Wealthy Student
www.wealthystudent.co.uk

Weanie Beans

1   Do something you love

You will be living and breathing your job 24 hours a day. If you choose a trade you don't have a passion for, you will grow to resent working and everything you do for it will become infinitely harder. However. if you choose to work in a field you love, that passion will not fail to come across to your customers, and your enthusiasm will rub off on your staff.

2   Be prepared to fail

Because you will. Whether it's losing track of your paperwork, missing out on a big job because you were too late/disorganised/unprepared, or even if your first start-up falls flat on its face – how can you improve if you don't have anything to improve on? Failure is a big motivator to prove to everyone how awesome you really are.

3   Learn how to use Excel

Coming from an Excel lover this might seem a bit much, but really Excel is your friend. Don't be afraid of it, because it will help keep you organised. When you're starting out, accountancy fees can be crippling to your finances – keep a simple spreadsheet with your money in/money out and receipts well organised and you'll find doing your tax return easy and simple. And if you are too afraid to do it yourself, you will have saved yourself a fortune on accounting fees by being able to hand over a USB stick with your finances on. An accountant should pay for his/herself, so if they're not saving you money (and we're not talking tax evasion here, just good account management) then you shouldn't be paying them.

4   Be prepared to work two jobs

As primarily a retail business, we were really lucky to be able to spend time testing the water in our early days. I started Weanie Beans when I was still in full-time employment. I had the security of a monthly salary whilst being able to build, then grow, a new business. The lost days off were worth their weight in gold as it meant I could take bigger risks without feeling the financial pinch.

5   Don't spend unnecessary money

When Weanie Beans started, it was just a name; no branding, no logo, no website. IT was just me, a lot of borrowed equipment, the cheapest food grade bags I could find and a sharpie pen to write the origin of the coffees on the bags. People didn't care – they knew I loved what I did, and that's what sold the products, not smart vinyl banners and professionally printed labels.

5   Take a day off

It's easy to get carried away when you're running your own business – you're constantly receiving emails, you're up until midnight working… We've all done it. I've learnt the hard way that there really is such a thing as too much work – and it's not a nice thing to learn. You CAN and MUST take a day off. Otherwise all that will happen is you'll start making mistakes that you'll need to rectify later.

6   Delegate

Yes, I know, the job will be done perfectly if you do it. And having exceptionally high standards is good, but not being able to delegate often means you don't trust your staff. Trust them to get it right, and if they make a mistake, they'll learn from it. You did.

Adeline Vining

Founder, Weanie Beans
www.weaniebeans.com

Jonny White

THE MOST IMPORTANT THING YOU CAN HAVE when starting and running a business is motivation; everything you need to make it a success will only come about with lots of motivation.

A good idea is important but lots of people come up with good ideas all of the time. An idea without motivation is worthless because it won't become a reality.

People often say, "It must be amazing being your own boss. If you want a day off you can have it". Whilst I agree that there are perks to being your own boss, if this is a key factor about why you want to set up your own business then you aren't motivated by the right things. Without someone telling you what to do on a day-to-day basis, you need to be able to tell yourself what to do and stay at it.

Motivation is essential but how do you stay motivated, and what should you do if you lose motivation? Everyone is different and it is important to recognise what motivates you to keep up momentum.

In the early days of setting up my business, motivation came easy. Everything was fresh and exciting, I could envisage the product and I was looking forward to getting something ready to start selling. I found it was important to make the most of my drive at this point and work really hard. It took about four months for me to prepare version one of my product that I could show to potential customers and over this time motivation started to dwindle.

There were of course certain tasks that I didn't enjoy and that took a long time, such as thinking about the terms and conditions that users had to agree to on sign up, or building the password recovery process. I found that interspersing some fun jobs really helped to keep me focussed on the end goal and keep a positive attitude to the project as a whole.

Eventually, I got too excited about the product I was building (or too bored building it) and decided to test the water by sending an email to two potential customers. One of them got back in touch and was very interested and wanted to become a paying customer right away. This gave me a much needed boost that helped me through the final stages and get something ready for market.

I also realised that my product didn't need to be perfect when I launched. My product was good enough for people to start using it and so I let people in. The response from the customers and PR continued the momentum and spurred me on to make the product better before letting more people in.

Once the product was officially launched we received a bit more press that helped generate more customers. There is nothing more motivating than the press saying nice things about you and having happy paying customers. I used this catalyst to find more customers.

I often lose motivation when I hit a brick wall or when I don't know how to proceed. In these scenarios, I buy a self-help book on whatever it is that causing a problem. When reading the book as soon as I find I am motivated to take on the challenge I put the book down and get to work. I have a lot of books that I have only read the first chapter of but they helped a great deal. If you are feeling motivated right now then put this book down and get some work done!

Jonny White

Founder, Ticket Tailor
www.jonnywhite.me

Wolds Target Accessories

Our inspiration

WE TRAVELLED 374 MILES TO BUY CLOTHING for our hobby. After liaising with the company for several weeks they had not got the items, even after assuring us they had. The customer service was appalling, not even offering a drink. On the way back Denise made a remark, "We could do better than that". After a few months of making plans we just went for it. I left my full-time job to concentrate on the business and my partner is at university doing a masters degree.

We had no business plan or strategy; it just felt like the right thing to do. We knew our customers and the equipment we needed. Not that we would recommend this was the right way but it has worked for us. As it happens we won a marketing competition so we now have a specialist team working with us.

How do you advertise the business?

We launched the business at the country's largest Shooting and Country show, a bit of a gamble as there had not been any other business that specialised in the type of equipment we supply there before. Our website was active but not complete but the interest was amazing.

I wrote an editorial for the local newspapers who loved the story; I also managed to get the editorial published in several national papers of which some are still running the story. The papers love a good story and we get far more custom from this than an advert.

We have joined some of the social networking sites which actually bring in business; these can be addictive so I limit the amount of time spent on them.

Is it possible to bring an idea into reality?

As our business started from our hobby we knew the difficulties of finding the right clothing, in particular for the ladies. We decided to design our own brand. Since winning the marketing competition the dream of doing this has now become a reality. The process of having them manufactured is underway with the garments being made in our home county and having a British label.

Running the business is hard work with long hours spent on it. We work from home and it's very hard not to keep checking the website etc. all night, having a cut-off time is important so make sure you stick to it. I also have a list of tasks each day, prioritise your workload and work through it even if you don't feel like it.

As yet we do not have premises but this enables us to keep the costs down until the business can sustain the extra costs.

It's early days and we are now in our fourth month of trading, the business is going the right way and we both have total confidence that it will continue to grow.

We are not experts in running a business and we will probably make mistakes. Mistakes are something we learn from so the key is not to become despondent but to carry on building your dream.

An ex student of mine once said, "Never let your fears take away your dreams". I always think that to myself when things get a little difficult.

Denise Popple

Partner, Wolds Target Accessories
www.woldstargetaccessories.co.uk

Work**A**round.me

IT'S ALWAYS GOOD TO WORK ON AN IDEA that you believe in. Leaving your job immediately to start a company is not important, as experts may agree. I worked on my start-up while having a full-time job, and left after a couple of months in order to focus on my start-up, WorkAround.me.

I'm not going talk about the do's and don'ts. Instead, I am just going to share my experiences with you.

Here is what I've learned so far:

1. It's never a one-man show. It's very important to have a great team and co-founder/s. Having an idea is one thing and executing it well is another. For this reason, a strong team is vital. However, finding the right team is the most difficult and important task.

2. No matter how seasoned or experience you are, you will need mentoring.

3. Sometimes you have to learn things on your own by reading books and blogs and doing research about start-ups (mistakes/why they fail, etc.). It's just a case of getting your hands dirty.

4. A start-up can be more emotionally draining than most other endeavours. You feel guilty when you're doing things for pleasure instead of using that time to build your company. It can be an emotional roller-coaster of hope and despair.

5. Having said that, every day is different and exciting. The feeling that comes from customers using your product/service and appreciating them is unmatched.

6. Don't waste too much time and energy in getting your start-up listed/mentioned on tech sites. They can be a good way to gain visibility among investors and the tech community in general, but in my experience, it didn't have value beyond that.

7. Meeting with other start-ups and sharing ideas is always fun. It's easy to leverage the knowledge you gain from bouncing ideas; their enthusiasm and energy is infectious.

Chances are, more often than not, your first start-up may fail. However, the knowledge and experience you gain will allow you to expose yourself to future opportunities and safeguard yourself against future failures.

All the best.

Devang Chouhan

Founder, WorkAround.me

Young Guns

Dear Entrepreneur,

IN 2005, MY BROTHER AND I set up a music company from a bedroom in South London with nothing but a £1,500 overdraft and a mission. We noticed that musicians were graduating from top music colleges with little idea about how to market themselves and that few were effectively harnessing their talent. We seized the opportunity to link artists with the music and event industries and Young Guns was born.

Looking back, growing organically whilst working within our means is the best strategy we could have followed. We developed an ethos where we would never report a financial loss and we found our feet naturally. We had some exciting achievements, including signing bands in major deals to record companies, creating entertainment experiences for over 2,000 exclusive parties, taking bands all over the world but we made mistakes along the way too.

It is easy to glamorise entrepreneurship. So, below are some no-nonsense practical tips that either helped us or could have saved us money – and perhaps they could spell the difference between success and failure for you:

When starting out, align your business around three parameters:

1.   Identify your passion and create a business in a related field

2.   Incorporate your own core skillset or a unique perspective

3.   Choose a sector where there is significant potential

By drawing on our musical backgrounds we gained a natural advantage that gave us credibility when bringing new bands and shows to market. It also means we love what we do and the scope for potential is limitless.

- **Choosing your business partner.** In the initial stages of creating a company, the brand is incredibly fragile. If you choose a business partner, choose well. I work with my brother; we have exactly the same vision and scale of ambition.

- **Building your team.** Be honest with yourself about your strengths and weaknesses. This way you can build a team with a balanced skillset, allowing you to focus your time in ways that will deliver the greatest impact. We have hired people we respect and admire. Don't grow your team too big too fast. Managing a smaller quality team has yielded greater results for us; we are leaner and more efficient as a result.

- **Managing your finances.** Having strict payment terms, thus minimising your exposure, could be the making or breaking of your company. When we started out, we were soon owed over £250,000 by overdue debtors. Taking on a brilliant bookkeeper has been worth its weight in gold (and nothing is more sobering than losing money that is owed to you). This will also help with your forecasting, managing your cash flow and planning effectively.

- **PR is important.** Winning business awards from HSBC Start-Up Stars, NatWest Startups Awards, Ernst & Young's Entrepreneur program and other industry awards has helped put us on the map.

- **Think big.** Do not be scared to think big but don't delay in taking action. We launched on a tour bus with our orchestra supporting McFly. From this, we quickly formed Escala who we subsequently signed to Simon Cowell's label, Syco.

- **Hire a good lawyer.** We have saved tens of thousands of pounds and gained superb advice by choosing our lawyers well.

- **Selling**. When approaching a prospective client, always approach with an idea in mind. That is what excites people and makes them receptive to you; this is how we get the attention of record industry executives. If you don't have an idea already, come up with one!

- **Take a holiday**. The pressures involved in setting up a business can be overwhelming at first so it is important to step away periodically to remind yourself why you fell in love with your business.

- **Quality**. Aspire to the highest standards. Our ethos is not to accept anything but the best and clients have come to expect this from us.

- **Mentors**. We found it useful to have mentors. You can even formalise this, as many companies do, and create an advisory board. A surprising number of very successful people will be happy to sit on this board.

- **Evolve**. Constantly be aware of your competitors. If your offering becomes irrelevant, a competitor changes the game, or the market moves, then you need to adapt. Since the global recession, our market (in luxury entertainment) has changed and we have found that our creativity is our core asset. This spurred us on to partner with companies to create entertainment experiences that are inspiring, original and groundbreaking. We now create acts and shows that we own (or co-own) and have a more robust business model as a result. Young Guns has become the leading UK entertainment company in the event industry and main provider of young talent in the music industry.

- **Say thank you**. We often hold parties on our Mayfair roof terrace to thank our clients and suppliers in equal measure. Showing appreciation to those around you on a daily basis is very important.

- And finally, **listen to advice but go with your gut** – most of the time you already know the answer!

Dominic Lyon

Founder, Young Guns UK

www.younggunsuk.com

Zac and Mo

What would you advise yourself if you could go back to the day you started your business?

Just got for it! And start as soon as you can after leaving school or college. Make the most of living at home and by the time you're in your early 20s, you will hopefully have built a strong business and may never have to work for anyone else again!

What inspired you to start a business?

The freedom to make our own decisions and to drive things forward without going through layers of management. Although it sounds a bit corny, we also had a dream to create something of our own.

Why start a business and not work for someone else?

Everyone is different and for many people working as part of a larger organisation suits them. It gives them routine, a good salary, and boundaries to work within. For others it doesn't work at all! If you are someone who likes a challenge, likes the freedom to dream and likes the idea of leaving your mark on the world, don't work for someone else. Work for yourself!

Is it possible to start from scratch?

Absolutely, we did. But bear in mind that the smaller you start, the longer it will take you to grow. Make sure you surround yourself with supportive people and find a way to stay motivated. We like to read about other people's success, it helps to keep us focused and gives us something to aim for.

Do you have any daily routines that make things run smoother?

Although working for yourself allows you to be flexible, we find a bit of structure to the day is useful. As a small business we're juggling so many different tasks that it's easy to forget something important. We check our website and social media channels at the beginning of every day to make sure everything is running as it should. Once we know the 'shop front' is ok, we can focus on 'stockroom' jobs.

Jamie Paterson and Louise Elliott

Founders, Zac and Mo
www.zacandmo.com

Zigwagz

From street market to Harrods!

I HAD BEEN WORKING ON LUCRATIVE Governed and European Funded contracts since the 1990s but that all changed on the 31st March 2011. I suddenly found myself contractless as the Government pulled all funding pending the delivery of a new programme.

I had been managing and running training courses and seminars for unemployed customers, offering them a positive approach to their job search, mentoring and providing advice and guidance as well as encouraging them to open their minds to new markets and consider self-employment as an option as the economy changed.

Now it was my turn to rethink my career. I had to take a totally new approach to my future. In line with the Mary Portas review I researched the possibility of retail but knew the funds were not available to open a shop on the high street. I had seen leather dog collars being sold in Spain and decided I too could do something with this idea and there was born the concept of ZigwagZ collars. I bought fabulously soft leather from Spain and started selling basic designs on Sheringham Market. I met some great people, sold a lot of collars and got a wonderful Norfolk tan. This was a fabulous place to work in the height of summer but come the autumn I struggled to sell enough to sustain any form of lifestyle!

Following a discussion with my daughter's headteacher who suggested I approach Harrods I went about creating new designs and emailed images to the buyer for the pet department. Within 20 minutes of sending the email I received a reply asking me to attend a meeting the following day! I was so excited and my first order came through whilst I was on the train on the way home from the meeting!! I kept pinching myself!!

From street market to Harrods – a fantastic result! Harrods now place an order each month and my collars are selling well. Their name alone has opened doors and I now have my collars in a number of retail outlets and am currently in conversation with two big names. My collars have been featured on ITV's *This Morning*, are worn and loved by celebrities' dogs, and I've been interviewed on the radio and featured in the press.

It has been great. Having studied art at university and had a sales and marketing based career I find myself in an unenvied position of utilising both my skills and passion every day. And with the added benefit of working from home around the needs of my three children. I would thoroughly recommend others to look at new markets, believe in themselves and follow their dreams. Life is good in the world of ZigwagZ collars.

Sharon Pomeroy

Founder, ZigwagZ
www.zigwagz.biz

Dear Entrepreneur,

CONGRATULATIONS ON CONSIDERING starting your own business! However, the desire to be successful is the first and most important step. In order to achieve your goals you need not only motivation but also the desire to work hard, the ability to turn each hurdle into a challenge and the humility to learn from your mistakes.

I always had a passion for sport and was a nationally ranked junior swimmer and runner who discovered triathlon at Loughborough. In 2006 I became the World Biathle Champion and World Amateur Aquathlon Champion. The same year I graduated with a First Class degree in Architectural Engineering and won a prize in the Loughborough University Business Plan competition. This encouraged me to work at the Loughborough Innovation Centre where I developed my own sports brand, Zone3.

My main suggestions for how to be a successful entrepreneur are as follows:

- Try to start your business in an area you know about and understand. You need your business to grow slowly and steadily. Re-invest your profits in the company and keep a close eye on finances and cash-flow.

- Don't be afraid to try out different ideas to see what works and what doesn't. Don't invest in production until you feel confident your products have a place in your market area. Make some prototypes and see how customers react – modify and adapt your product as necessary. This could potentially take months and months but it is worth it rather than releasing a product which not up to scratch.

- Start with low-cost items and profitability until you feel confident enough to invest in higher priced items. Know your marketplace and what your customers need and always strive to be better than the competition. Be flexible and innovative and use your customer feedback to improve and modify your products. Without your customers you do not have a business – they are your company's greatest asset.

- If designing a new product, quality and performance always has to come first. Your sales and marketing efforts will only be successful if you are offering top quality items. Take time to make the very best products possible and only think about introducing them to the marketplace when you are fully confident in the quality of your product. During the present economic 'gloom' be competitive with prices, this can help you win your market share against much bigger companies.

Starting your own business is very exciting but can also be daunting due to the uncertain outcome and risk involved. However, owning your company offers the opportunity to be your own boss, to produce goods, have your own brand and to watch the small company you formed move forward and grow. There may be difficulties but with commitment, hard work, motivation and perseverance you have a very high chance of being successful.

Good Luck!

James Lock

Founder, Zone3
www.RaceZone3.com

Final note

So, what have we learned?

APART FROM THE EXTREMELY VALUABLE practical advice contained in this book it seems like the most important thing is to JUST GO FOR IT! I'm sure many of you reading this would have spent years wanting to go it alone and become your own boss, to have the freedom of working for yourself and creating your own destiny. Remember that quote:

66 A journey of a thousand miles begins with a single step. 99

– Lao Tzu

Put something in place, buy that domain name, buy a market stall, get an invoice book, do some market research, speak to people that have done what you want to do, work 5-9, send emails to prospective clients, get connected on LinkedIn, create a Facebook page, get followers on Twitter...Just do **something** to get started and then take a few more steps. It doesn't seem such a daunting task if you break it down.

Nowadays with the internet anyone can start a business from their own home and with tiny start up costs, for example, we set up a Twitter account and within two months had over 10,000 followers (that's the circulation of a small magazine) and it's still growing. By the time this book is published we hope to have well over 20,000 followers. All it cost us to get to this point is persistence, attitude, time and hard work.

Persistence – If you want something you are going to have to expect rejections, complications and general problems that will slow you down. As long as you are persistent you will succeed.

Attitude – This goes hand in hand with persistence. With the right attitude you won't let anything get in your way. You will ignore the naysayers and remember why you started.

Time – If you want it bad enough you will work all the hours you have, your sleep will change from eight hours to four to gain time. You will be working from your mobile at family meals. You will make time to succeed.

Hard work – You will not get anywhere in life if you do the bare minimum and just coast. You have to go above and beyond your call of duty. You have to work when you don't want to. If you can honestly say 'I will work my hardest' then you will succeed.

To be honest, all I am saying above is what I tell myself. Like I said at the beginning of this book, I am the same as you, I haven't started a business and I haven't left the 9-5. What I am saying above is what we need to remind ourselves if we want to succeed. All I have said in this section is what the 70+ business owners that have written in this book have said and also what they have been through to get where they are today.

The best lessons you will learn are those that hurt the most, don't be scared to make mistakes, make them and use them to your advantage and learn from them.

We'd like to thank EVERY SINGLE contributor who helped make this happen.

Yours truly,

Danny and Andrew

eBook
edition

As a buyer of the print edition of *Dear Entrepreneur* you can now download the eBook edition free of charge to read on an eBook reader, your smartphone or your computer. Simply go to:

http://ebooks.harriman-house.com/dearentrepreneur

or point your smartphone at the QR code below.

You can then register and download your eBook copy of the book.

www.brightwordpublishing.co.uk

CPSIA information can be obtained at www.ICGtesting.com
Printed in the USA
LVOW121500020513

332035LV00018B/1028/P